MINCE
in MINUTES

THE AUSTRALIAN
Women's Weekly

contents

If you're strapped for time, strapped for cash and strapped for inspiration, meet your new best friend: mince. We've covered all bases in this book, from the old favourites like spaghetti and meatballs, to mince with an Asian slant, yummy burgers and even tasty Middle Eastern mince meals. So whether you're already a fan or a newcomer to the wonderful world of mince, I'm sure that you'll soon discover why we're so excited about these recipes; your family and friends are sure to be pleased with them, too.

Pamela Clark

Food Director

gourmet beef burgers

preparation time 15 minutes **cooking time** 10 minutes **serves** 4

Mesclun, also known as mixed greens or spring salad mix, is a blend of assorted young lettuce and other green leaves, including baby spinach leaves, mizuna and curly endive.

750g beef mince

1 cup (70g) stale breadcrumbs

2 tablespoons finely chopped fresh flat-leaf parsley

2 tablespoons sun-dried tomato paste

125g mozzarella cheese, thinly sliced

½ cup (150g) mayonnaise

4 bread rolls

50g mesclun

1 small red onion (100g), thinly sliced

2 tablespoons drained, sliced sun-dried tomatoes in oil

1   Combine beef, breadcrumbs, parsley and 1½ tablespoons of the paste in large bowl. Using hands, shape mixture into four patties.

2   Cook patties on heated oiled barbecue, uncovered, until browned and cooked through. Top patties with cheese; cook until cheese melts.

3   Combine remaining paste and mayonnaise in small bowl.

4   Split rolls in half. Place each half cut-side down onto barbecue; cook until lightly toasted.

5   Sandwich patties, mayonnaise mixture, mesclun, onion and sliced tomatoes between bread rolls.
    PER SERVING *39.2g fat; 3219kJ (770 cal)*

BURGERS

beef and silver beet burgers

preparation time 15 minutes (plus standing time) cooking time 25 minutes serves 4

½ cup (80g) burghul

1kg silver beet, trimmed

750g beef mince

1 medium brown onion (150g), finely chopped

1 clove garlic, crushed

1 tablespoon cajun seasoning

TOMATO RELISH

2 teaspoons vegetable oil

1 small brown onion (80g), finely chopped

415g can crushed tomatoes

130g can corn kernels, drained

¼ cup (50g) firmly packed brown sugar

¼ cup (60ml) white vinegar

1 Cover burghul with cold water; stand 30 minutes, drain.
2 Boil, steam or microwave silver beet until just wilted; drain. Squeeze excess liquid from silver beet; chop roughly.
3 Using hands, combine burghul and silver beet in large bowl with beef, onion, garlic and seasoning. Form mixture into 12 rissole shapes; set aside on tray. (Can be made ahead to this stage. Cover, and refrigerate overnight or freeze.)
4 Cook rissoles, in batches, in large heated oiled pan until browned both sides and cooked through. Serve rissoles with tomato relish.
   TOMATO RELISH Heat oil in medium pan; cook onion, stirring, until soft. Add undrained tomatoes, corn, sugar and vinegar; stir over low heat until sugar dissolves. Bring to boil; simmer, uncovered, stirring occasionally, about 25 minutes or until relish thickens. (Can be made a day ahead. Cover and refrigerate overnight, or freeze.)
   PER SERVING *16.6g fat; 2123kJ (508 cal)*

mexican burgers

preparation time 20 minutes cooking time 10 minutes serves 6

750g beef mince

310g can kidney beans, rinsed, drained

4 green onions, finely chopped

2 fresh red thai chillies, seeded, finely chopped

1 teaspoon hot paprika

1 tablespoon tomato paste

6 hamburger buns

6 butter lettuce leaves

1 small avocado (200g), mashed

½ cup (120g) sour cream

2 tablespoons lemon juice

1 Combine beef, beans, onion, chilli, paprika and paste in medium bowl. Using hands, shape mixture into six patties.
2 Cook patties on heated oiled barbecue, uncovered, until well-browned and cooked through.
3 Split buns in half. Place each half cut-side down onto barbecue; cook until lightly toasted.
4 Top base of buns with lettuce, patties and combined avocado, sour cream, and juice. Replace top of buns, if desired.
   PER SERVING *26.9g fat; 2098kJ (502 cal)*

burgers with mustard mayonnaise

preparation time 20 minutes **cooking time** 15 minutes **serves** 4

500g beef mince

½ cup (40g) packaged seasoned stuffing mix

¼ cup (60ml) tomato sauce

¼ cup coarsely chopped fresh flat-leaf parsley

2 large white onions (400g), thinly sliced

4 hamburger buns

8 green oak leaf lettuce leaves

1 large tomato (250g), thinly sliced

1 tablespoon seeded mustard

½ cup (150g) mayonnaise

1 Combine beef, stuffing mix, sauce and parsley in medium bowl. Using hands, shape mixture into four patties.

2 Cook patties on heated oiled barbecue, uncovered, until browned and cooked through.

3 Meanwhile, cook sliced onion on heated oiled barbecue plate until soft and browned.

4 Split buns in half. Place each half cut-side down onto barbecue; cook until lightly toasted.

5 Top base of buns with lettuce, tomato, patties, combined mustard and mayonnaise, then onion; replace top of buns.

PER SERVING *26.6g fat; 2322kJ (556 cal)*

pork chutney burgers

preparation time 20 minutes cooking time 10 minutes serves 4

500g pork mince

1 cup (100g) packaged breadcrumbs

1 egg, lightly beaten

1 tablespoon finely chopped fresh flat-leaf parsley

2 tablespoons fruit chutney

2 tablespoons grated cheddar cheese

4 hamburger buns

2 lettuce leaves, shredded

1 medium tomato (190g), thinly sliced

4 canned pineapple rings

1   Combine pork, breadcrumbs, egg and parsley in medium bowl. Using hands, shape mixture into four patties; flatten slightly. Indent centres; spoon combined chutney and cheese into centre of each patty. Shape patties around chutney and cheese to enclose mixture; flatten slightly.

2   Cook patties on heated oiled barbecue, uncovered, until browned and cooked through.

3   Split buns in half. Place each half cut-side down onto barbecue; cook until lightly toasted.

4   Top base of buns with lettuce, tomato, pineapple and patties; top with extra chutney, if desired. Replace top of buns.
    PER SERVING *14.6g fat; 2096kJ (502 cal)*

lamb and burghul sausages

preparation time 30 minutes (plus standing and refrigeration time) cooking time 10 minutes serves 4

½ cup (80g) burghul

750g lamb mince

¼ cup finely chopped fresh flat-leaf parsley

2 tablespoons finely chopped fresh mint

1 tablespoon grated lemon rind

2 medium tomatoes (380g), peeled, finely chopped

1 tablespoon ground cumin

1 tablespoon ground coriander

2 cloves garlic, crushed

½ cup (35g) stale breadcrumbs

1 egg, lightly beaten

2 large brown onions (400g), thinly sliced

1 cup (240g) sour cream

1   Place burghul in small bowl and cover with cold water. Let stand 15 minutes, then drain.

2   Rinse burghul under cold water; drain. Squeeze to remove excess moisture.

3   Combine burghul in large bowl with lamb, parsley, mint, rind, tomato, cumin, coriander, garlic, breadcrumbs and egg. Using hands, shape ¼-cup measures of the mixture into sausages. Cover and refrigerate for three hours or overnight.

4   Cook sausages on heated oiled barbecue, uncovered, until browned all over and cooked through.

5   Meanwhile, cook onion on heated barbecue until browned. Serve sausages with onion and sour cream. Accompany with bread and mixed lettuce leaves, if desired.
    PER SERVING *44.9g fat; 2968kJ (710 cal)*

lamb kofta with chilli and yogurt sauces

preparation time 20 minutes cooking time 10 minutes serves 6

1kg lean lamb mince

1 large brown onion (200g), finely chopped

1 clove garlic, crushed

1 tablespoon ground cumin

2 teaspoons ground turmeric

2 teaspoons ground allspice

1 tablespoon finely chopped fresh mint

2 tablespoons finely chopped fresh
flat-leaf parsley

1 egg, lightly beaten

6 pocket pitta, quartered

YOGURT SAUCE

¾ cup (200g) low-fat yogurt

1 clove garlic, crushed

1 tablespoon finely chopped fresh
flat-leaf parsley

CHILLI TOMATO SAUCE

¼ cup (60ml) tomato sauce

¼ cup (60ml) chilli sauce

1 Using hands, combine lamb, onion, garlic, spices, herbs and egg in large bowl; shape mixture into 18 balls. Mould balls around skewers to form sausage shapes. Cook, in batches, on heated oiled grill plate (or grill or barbecue) until browned all over and cooked through.

2 Serve kofta with pitta, yogurt sauce and chilli tomato sauce. Serve with tabbouleh, if desired.
 YOGURT SAUCE Combine ingredients in small bowl.
 CHILLI TOMATO SAUCE Combine sauces in small bowl.
 PER SERVING *14.5g fat; 1817kJ (435 cal)*

TIPS You will need 18 bamboo skewers for this recipe. Soak skewers in water for at least an hour before use, to prevent them from splintering or scorching.
Kofta can be finger-, ball- or torpedo-shaped, but all are made of minced meat and spices, then hand-moulded before grilling.

chicken and ham burgers

preparation time 15 minutes cooking time 10 minutes serves 6

1kg chicken mince

250g sliced ham, finely chopped

2 tablespoons finely chopped fresh coriander

1 clove garlic, crushed

3 green onions, chopped finely

1 cup (70g) stale breadcrumbs

¼ cup (60ml) olive oil

DIPPING SAUCE

2 tablespoons salt-reduced soy sauce

1 tablespoon sweet chilli sauce

1 Combine all ingredients, except the oil, in large bowl. Shape ¼-cups of mixture into flat patties.

2 Heat oil in medium frying pan; cook patties, in batches, until browned on both sides and cooked through.

3 Serve patties with dipping sauce, and rocket leaves, if desired.
DIPPING SAUCE Combine sauces in small bowl.
PER SERVING 25.3g fat; 1789kJ (427 cal)

TIP Patties can be prepared several hours ahead.

fish burgers

preparation time 15 minutes cooking time 20 minutes serves 4

600g firm white fish fillets, coarsely chopped

1 egg

¼ teaspoon sweet paprika

1 teaspoon ground cumin

1 teaspoon ground coriander

½ teaspoon garlic salt

40cm loaf turkish bread

2 lebanese cucumbers (260g)

¾ cup (210g) yogurt

1 tablespoon finely chopped fresh mint

1 Blend or process fish, egg, paprika, cumin, coriander and garlic salt until smooth. Using hands, shape mixture into four patties.

2 Cook patties on heated oiled barbecue, uncovered, until browned and cooked through.

3 Cut bread into four pieces; split each in half. Place each half cut-side down onto barbecue; cook until lightly toasted.

4 Using a vegetable peeler, slice cucumbers into thin strips.

5 Combine remaining ingredients in small bowl.

6 Top bread bases with patties; top with equal amounts of cucumber and yogurt mixture, then remaining bread.
PER SERVING 6.6g fat; 2193kJ (525 cal)

lamb burgers with tomato salsa

preparation time 30 minutes (plus standing and refrigeration time) cooking time 30 minutes serves 6

1 medium eggplant (300g)

coarse cooking salt

2 tablespoons olive oil

6 bread rolls

120g rocket

½ cup (40g) flaked parmesan cheese

PATTIES

600g lamb mince

1 medium brown onion (150g), finely chopped

2 cloves garlic, crushed

⅓ cup (50g) drained, finely chopped
sun-dried tomatoes in oil

⅓ cup (50g) seeded black olives, chopped

¾ cup (50g) stale breadcrumbs

2 tablespoons finely chopped fresh basil

1 egg, lightly beaten

TOMATO SALSA

1 large red capsicum (350g)

3 small tomatoes (390g), finely chopped

1 small red onion (100g), finely chopped

1 teaspoon balsamic vinegar

1 teaspoon finely chopped fresh oregano

1   Cut eggplant into 1.5cm slices; place in strainer. Sprinkle with salt; stand 30 minutes.
2   Rinse eggplant under cold running water; drain on absorbent paper. Brush eggplant with oil. Cook eggplant on heated oiled barbecue, uncovered, until browned both sides and tender.
3   Split rolls in half. Place each half cut-side down onto barbecue; cook until lightly toasted. Fill with eggplant, rocket, cheese, patties and tomato salsa.
PATTIES Combine ingredients in medium bowl; mix well. Using hands, shape mixture into six patties; place on tray. Cover; refrigerate 30 minutes. Cook patties on heated oiled barbecue, uncovered, until browned and cooked through.
TOMATO SALSA Quarter capsicum; remove seeds and membranes. Cook capsicum on heated oiled barbecue, skin-side down, until skin blisters and blackens. Cover capsicum pieces with plastic or paper for 5 minutes; peel away skin, slice capsicum thinly. Combine capsicum with remaining ingredients in medium bowl.
PER SERVING *22.4g fat; 2152kJ (515 cal)*

BURGERS

16

chicken burgers with avocado cream

preparation time 30 minutes cooking time 10 minutes serves 4

800g chicken mince

2 rashers lean bacon (140g), finely chopped

⅓ cup (25g) grated parmesan cheese

3 green onions, finely chopped

1 tablespoon finely chopped fresh thyme

1 egg, lightly beaten

½ cup (50g) packaged breadcrumbs

20cm square focaccia

1 cup (55g) snow pea sprouts

2 medium tomatoes (260g), thinly sliced

1 medium carrot (120g), thinly sliced

AVOCADO CREAM

1 medium avocado (250g), coarsely chopped

125g packaged cream cheese, softened

1 tablespoon lemon juice

1 Combine chicken, bacon, cheese, onion, thyme, egg and breadcrumbs in medium bowl. Using hands, shape mixture into four patties.

2 Cook patties on heated oiled barbecue, uncovered, until browned and cooked through.

3 Cut focaccia into four pieces; split each in half. Place each half cut-side down onto barbecue; cook until lightly toasted.

4 Top focaccia bases with sprouts, patties, tomato, carrot and a dollop of avocado cream.
   AVOCADO CREAM Combine ingredients in bowl; mash with a fork until well combined.
   PER SERVING *15.1g fat; 3473kJ (831 cal)*

cajun chicken burgers

preparation time 15 minutes cooking time 15 minutes serves 4

500g chicken mince

1 medium zucchini (120g), coarsely grated

1 medium carrot (120g), coarsely grated

2 tablespoons plain flour

2 teaspoons cajun seasoning

4 wholemeal bread rolls

2 medium tomatoes (380g), seeded, finely chopped

1 tablespoon finely chopped fresh chives

2 teaspoons olive oil

4 large lettuce leaves

⅓ cup (80ml) sour cream

¼ teaspoon hot paprika

1 Using hands, combine chicken, zucchini, carrot, flour and seasoning in large bowl; shape mixture into four patties. (Can be made ahead to this stage. Cover, and refrigerate overnight or freeze.) Cook patties in large heated oiled pan until browned both sides and cooked through.

2 Meanwhile, split rolls in half. Place each half cut-side down onto barbecue; cook until lightly toasted. Combine tomato, chives and oil in small bowl.

3 To serve, sandwich patties, lettuce, tomato mixture and combined sour cream and paprika between roll halves.
   PER SERVING *23.4g fat; 2236kJ (535 cal)*

sloppy joes

No one knows the origin of the name, but this American version of savoury mince is everybody's favourite.

1 tablespoon vegetable oil

2 medium brown onions (340g), finely chopped

1 small green capsicum (150g), finely chopped

1 trimmed celery stick (75g), finely chopped

750g beef mince

2 tablespoons American mustard

1 tablespoon dark brown sugar

2 tablespoons cider vinegar

1 cup (250ml) tomato sauce

6 hamburger buns

3 kosher dill pickles, sliced thinly

500g packaged coleslaw

1 Heat oil in large pan; cook onion, capsicum and celery, stirring, until onion is soft. Add beef; cook, stirring, until well browned. Stir in mustard, sugar, vinegar and sauce; bring to a boil. Reduce heat; simmer, covered, about 40 minutes or until slightly thickened.

2 Halve buns; lightly toast each half. Divide pickles among bun bases, top with sloppy joe mixture and coleslaw; cover with tops of buns. Serve remaining coleslaw separately as salad, if desired.
PER SERVING *17.4g fat; 2257kJ (540 cal)*

country-style burgers

500g beef mince

1 small onion (80g), grated

1 clove garlic, crushed

1 tablespoon barbecue sauce

1 tablespoon tomato sauce

1 tablespoon Worcestershire sauce

1 cup (70g) stale breadcrumbs

1 egg, lightly beaten

1 teaspoon finely chopped fresh thyme

2 tablespoons finely chopped fresh flat-leaf parsley

1 small tomato (130g), finely chopped

GLAZE

¼ cup (60ml) barbecue sauce

2 teaspoons Worcestershire sauce

1 Using hands, combine all ingredients in large bowl; shape into eight patties, about 7cm wide. Place patties around the edge of a large oiled shallow microwave-safe dish.

2 Brush patties with glaze; cook, uncovered, on HIGH (100%) about 7 minutes or until cooked through. Serve sprinkled with extra chopped parsley, if desired.
GLAZE Combine sauces in a small bowl.
PER SERVING *10.8g fat; 1392kJ (333 cal)*

beef, tomato and pea pies

preparation time 15 minutes (plus refrigeration time) **cooking time** 45 minutes (plus cooling time) **makes** 6

1 tablespoon vegetable oil

1 small brown onion (80g), finely chopped

300g beef mince

400g can crushed tomatoes

1 tablespoon tomato paste

2 tablespoons Worcestershire sauce

½ cup (125ml) beef stock

½ cup (60g) frozen peas

3 sheets ready-rolled puff pastry

1 egg, lightly beaten

1 Heat oil in large saucepan, add onion; cook, stirring, until softened. Add beef; cook, stirring, until changed in colour. Stir in undrained tomatoes, tomato paste, sauce and stock; bring to a boil. Reduce heat; simmer, uncovered, about 20 minutes or until sauce thickens. Stir in peas. Allow to cool.

2 Preheat oven to 200°C/180°C fan-forced. Oil a six-hole ¾-cup (180ml) texas muffin pan.

3 Cut two 13cm rounds from opposite corners of each pastry sheet; cut two 9cm rounds from remaining corners of each sheet. Place six large rounds in muffin pan holes to cover bases and sides; trim any excess pastry. Lightly prick bases with a fork; refrigerate for 30 minutes. Cover the six small rounds with a damp cloth.

4 Cover pastry-lined muffin pan holes with baking paper; fill holes with uncooked rice or dried beans. Bake, uncovered, 10 minutes; remove paper and rice. Cool.

5 Spoon beef filling into holes; brush edges with a little egg. Top pies with small pastry rounds; gently press around edges to seal.

6 Brush pies with remaining egg; bake, uncovered, about 15 minutes or until browned lightly. Stand 5 minutes in pan before serving with mashed potato, if desired.

PER SERVING *26.9g fat; 1887kJ (451 cal)*

TIPS The filling can be made a day ahead.
Pies are best cooked close to serving.

PIES & PASTRIES

individual cheese and spinach meatloaves

preparation time 15 minutes cooking time 15 minutes serves 4

150g spinach, coarsely chopped

2 tablespoons water

2 tablespoons barbecue sauce

750g beef mince

½ cup (35g) stale breadcrumbs

3 green onions, finely chopped

1 tablespoon tomato paste

1 teaspoon seasoned pepper

½ teaspoon garlic powder

40g cheddar cheese, cut into quarters

1 Place spinach and the water in medium microwave-safe bowl, cook, covered, on HIGH (100%) 2 minutes, drain. Squeeze excess liquid from spinach; shred finely.
2 Brush four 1-cup (250ml) microwave-safe dishes with half of the barbecue sauce. Using hands, combine beef, breadcrumbs, onion, paste, pepper and powder in large bowl; shape into four patties. Make a hollow in the centre of each patty, push one-quarter of the spinach and a cube of cheese into centre of each patty; shape into round patties to enclose filling completely. Press into prepared dishes. Spread remaining barbecue sauce over top of patties.
3 Cook, uncovered, on MEDIUM-HIGH (70%) about 12 minutes or until firm. Stand, covered, 5 minutes, drain away liquid; turn out patties. Serve with fettuccine, if desired.
   PER SERVING *16.8g fat, 1572kJ (376 cal)*

bubble and squeak pie

preparation time 15 minutes cooking time 1 hour serves 4

2 teaspoons vegetable oil

1 large brown onion (200g), coarsely chopped

2 cloves garlic, crushed

500g beef mince

2 tablespoons tomato sauce

2 tablespoons Worcestershire sauce

1 tablespoon barbecue sauce

1 beef stock cube

1 cup (165g) cooked corn kernels

1 cup (180g) coarsely chopped cooked potatoes

1 cup (160g) coarsely chopped cooked pumpkin

½ cup (100g) coarsely chopped cooked carrot

¼ cup (30g) coarsely grated cheddar cheese

TOPPING

1 large potato (300g), coarsely chopped

300g pumpkin, coarsely chopped

40g butter

¼ cup (30g) coarsely grated cheddar cheese

1 Heat oil in large pan, cook onion and garlic, stirring, until onion is soft. Add beef; cook, stirring, until well browned. Stir in combined sauces, stock cube and 1 cup water; bring to a boil. Simmer, covered, 20 minutes. Add combined corn, potato, pumpkin and carrot; mix well. (Can be made ahead to this stage. Cover; refrigerate overnight.)
2 Preheat oven to 200°C/180°C fan-forced.
3 Spoon beef mixture into shallow 2-litre (8-cup capacity) oiled ovenproof baking dish. Spread topping over beef mixture; sprinkle with the cheese. Bake, uncovered, about 30 minutes or until browned and hot.
   TOPPING Boil, steam or microwave potato and pumpkin until tender; drain. Place potato and pumpkin in medium pan; mash over low heat until smooth. Stir in butter and cheese, cook, stirring, until butter and cheese melt and mixture is smooth.
   PER SERVING *26.8g fat; 2575kJ (616 cal)*

TIP For this recipe, you will need five cooked tiny new potatoes, one 200g piece cooked pumpkin, and one medium cooked carrot.

chilli con carne pie

preparation time 35 minutes (plus refrigeration time) cooking time 1 hour serves 6

1 tablespoon vegetable oil

1 large brown onion (200g), coarsely chopped

2 cloves garlic, crushed

2 teaspoons ground cumin

1 tablespoon mexican chilli powder

1kg beef mince

400g can crushed tomatoes

¼ cup (60ml) tomato paste

1 cup (250ml) water

420g can kidney beans, drained

¾ cup (180ml) sour cream

PASTRY

2 cups (300g) plain flour

150g butter, chopped

¼ cup (30g) coarsely grated cheddar cheese

2 tablespoons finely chopped chives

1 egg yolk

2 tablespoons cold water, approximately

1 egg, lightly beaten

1 Make pastry.
2 Meanwhile, heat oil in large pan; cook onion and garlic, stirring, until onion is soft. Add cumin and chilli powder; cook, stirring, until fragrant. Add beef; cook, stirring, until well browned. Add undrained tomatoes, paste, the water and beans; simmer, uncovered, about 30 minutes or until mixture thickens, cool.
3 Pour beef mixture into pastry case; top with pastry shapes. Bake, uncovered, about 15 minutes or until heated through. Serve with sour cream.
   PASTRY Grease 2-litre (8-cup capacity) ovenproof dish. Process flour and butter until just crumbly; add cheese, chives, egg yolk and enough water to make ingredients just cling together. Knead dough on floured surface until smooth, cover with plastic wrap; refrigerate 30 minutes. Reserve a quarter of the pastry; cover with plastic wrap. Roll remaining pastry on floured surface until large enough to line prepared dish. Lift pastry into dish, ease into side; trim edges. Cover; refrigerate 30 minutes. Roll reserved pastry on floured surface until 5mm thick; cut out shapes with cutter. Place pastry shapes on greased oven tray, cover; refrigerate 30 minutes. Preheat oven to 200°C/180°C fan-forced. Cover pastry-lined dish with baking paper; cover base with dried beans or rice. Place on oven tray; bake, uncovered, 10 minutes. Remove and discard paper and beans, return dish to oven; bake, uncovered, 10 minutes or until browned lightly; cool. Brush pastry shapes with egg; bake, uncovered, about 10 minutes or until browned lightly. Remove from oven; reduce oven temperature to 180°C/160°C fan-forced.
   PER SERVING 51.7g fat; 3616kJ (865 cal)

mediterranean meatloaf

preparation time 15 minutes (plus standing time) cooking time 1 hour 15 minutes serves 4

1kg beef mince

1 small brown onion (80g), finely chopped

2 cloves garlic, crushed

¼ cup (60ml) tomato paste

¼ cup (40g) coarsely chopped black olives

1 teaspoon dried oregano

1 tablespoon finely chopped fresh
flat-leaf parsley

¼ cup (20g) finely grated parmesan cheese

1 cup (70g) stale breadcrumbs

1 egg

¼ cup (60ml) tomato sauce

2 teaspoons Worcestershire sauce

TOMATO GRAVY

2 teaspoons olive oil

1 small (80g) brown onion, finely chopped

415g can crushed tomatoes

1 tablespoon gravy mix

1 Preheat oven to 180°C/160°C fan-forced.

2 Combine beef, onion, garlic, paste, olives, herbs, cheese, breadcrumbs and egg in large bowl; mix well. Press mixture into 14cm x 21cm loaf pan.

3 Bake, uncovered, 45 minutes. Brush top of meatloaf with combined sauces; bake, uncovered, about 30 minutes or until cooked through. Drain juices from pan; stand 5 minutes before slicing. (Can be made a day ahead. Cover; refrigerate overnight.) Serve meatloaf with tomato gravy.
   TOMATO GRAVY Heat oil in small pan; cook onion, stirring, until soft. Add undrained tomatoes and blended gravy mix and ½ cup water; simmer, stirring, until thickened. (Can be made a day ahead. Cover; refrigerate overnight.)
   PER SERVING *23.6g fat; 2370kJ (567 cal)*

bacon and beef loaf with plum sauce

preparation time 15 minutes cooking time 20 minutes serves 4

cooking-oil spray

6 rindless bacon rashers (390g)

500g beef mince

1 small onion (80g), finely chopped

1 small carrot (70g), coarsely grated

2 eggs, lightly beaten

1 tablespoon tomato paste

130g can creamed corn

1 cup (70g) stale breadcrumbs

1 tablespoon finely chopped fresh
flat-leaf parsley

PLUM SAUCE

½ cup (125ml) plum sauce

½ cup (125ml) beef stock

1 Coat 12cm x 21cm microwave-safe dish with cooking-oil spray; line base and sides with overlapping bacon rashers.

2 Using hands, combine beef, onion, carrot, egg, paste, corn, breadcrumbs and parsley in large bowl; press firmly over bacon in dish. Fold ends of bacon over meatloaf.

3 Cook, uncovered, on HIGH (100%) 20 minutes; drain away excess fat halfway through cooking. Stand, covered, 5 minutes before serving with plum sauce.
   PLUM SAUCE Combine ingredients in microwave-safe jug. Cook, uncovered, on HIGH (100%) 1 minute.
   PER SERVING *5.8g fat; 606kJ (145)*

meat and vegetable samosas

preparation time 1 hour 20 minutes (plus standing time) cooking time 30 minutes makes 28

1½ cups (225g) plain flour

2 teaspoons salt

2 tablespoons vegetable oil

⅓ cup (80ml) warm water, approximately

vegetable oil, for deep-frying

CHILLI, MINT AND BEEF FILLING

2 tablespoons vegetable oil

1 medium onion (150g), finely chopped

2 cloves garlic, crushed

2 teaspoons grated fresh ginger

½ teaspoon dried chilli flakes

2 teaspoons ground coriander

2 teaspoons garam masala

1 teaspoon ground turmeric

1 teaspoon sweet paprika

500g beef mince

2 tablespoons lemon juice

¼ cup finely chopped fresh mint

KUMARA AND CORIANDER FILLING

3 small kumaras (750g)

1 tablespoon vegetable oil

1 medium brown onion (150g), finely chopped

2 teaspoons cumin seeds

½ teaspoon black mustard seeds

1 long green chilli, finely chopped

2 cloves garlic, crushed

2 teaspoons grated fresh ginger

¼ teaspoon ground nutmeg

1 tablespoon lime juice

¼ cup finely chopped fresh coriander

1 Sift flour and salt into medium bowl; make well in the centre of flour, then add the 2 tablespoons of oil with just enough water to make a firm dough.

2 Knead dough on floured surface until smooth and elastic; form into a ball. Cover with plastic wrap; stand at room temperature for 30 minutes.

3 Meanwhile, make chilli, mint and beef filling or make kumara and coriander filling.

4 Divide dough into 14 equal pieces; roll each piece into a 14cm x 20cm oval, then cut oval in half widthways. Repeat process, keeping the remaining pieces covered to prevent drying out.

5 Brush edges of each half-oval with a little water; fold into cone shape. Fill with heaped tablespoon of filling; press edges together to seal. Repeat with remaining dough and filling.

6 Deep-fry samosas in hot oil, in batches, until browned and crisp; drain on absorbent paper.
CHILLI, MINT AND BEEF FILLING Heat oil in large frying pan; cook onion, stirring, until browned lightly. Add garlic, ginger, chilli and spices; cook, stirring, until fragrant. Add beef; cook, stirring, until well browned. Remove from heat, stir in juice and mint; cool.
KUMARA AND CORIANDER FILLING Cook whole kumaras until just tender, drain; cool. Cut each kumara into 1cm pieces. Heat oil in frying pan; cook onion, stirring, until soft. Add seeds, chilli, garlic, ginger and nutmeg; cook, stirring, until fragrant. Remove from heat, stir in kumara, juice and coriander; cool.
PER MEAT SAMOSA *10g fat; 627kJ (150 cal)*
PER VEGETABLE SAMOSA *6.3g fat; 493kJ (118 cal)*

TIP Each filling makes 28 samosas. Choose whichever filling you prefer, or make double the pastry recipe and use both fillings for variety.

meatloaf with caramelised onion

preparation time 15 minutes cooking time 1 hour serves 4

1 medium brown onion (150g), coarsely chopped

1 large carrot (180g), coarsely chopped

1 trimmed celery stick (75g), coarsely chopped

1 clove garlic, quartered

1 cup (150g) packaged breadcrumbs

2 teaspoons mustard powder

750g beef mince

2 eggs, lightly beaten

2 tablespoons mild chilli sauce

1½ tablespoons barbecue sauce

½ cup (125ml) tomato sauce

20g butter

3 medium brown onions (450g), thinly sliced, extra

2 tablespoons brown sugar

2 tablespoons cider vinegar

1 Preheat oven to 180°C/160°C fan-forced.

2 Blend or process onion, carrot, celery and garlic until chopped finely; place in large bowl. Add breadcrumbs, mustard powder, beef, egg and half of each sauce; using hands, mix until just combined.

3 Place beef mixture on lightly oiled swiss roll pan; with hands, form into a 10cm x 30cm loaf shape.

4 Brush top of meatloaf with half of remaining combined sauces. Bake, uncovered, brushing top occasionally with remaining combined sauces, about 1 hour or until cooked through.

5 Meanwhile, melt butter in large heavy-based saucepan; cook extra onion, stirring, about 10 minutes or until onion is soft and browned lightly. Stir in sugar and vinegar; cook, stirring, about 15 minutes or until onion is caramelised.

6 Serve meatloaf with caramelised onion, and mashed potato, if desired.
   PER SERVING *25.9g fat; 2689kJ (643 cal)*

   TIP Meatloaf can be prepared a day ahead and refrigerated, covered, or frozen for up to three months.

homemade sausage rolls

preparation time 30 minutes cooking time 45 minutes makes 16

2 large potatoes (600g), quartered

2 teaspoons vegetable oil

1 large brown onion (200g), grated

2 cloves garlic, crushed

1 teaspoon ground cumin

1 teaspoon curry powder

300g sausage mince

200g beef mince

4 sheets ready-rolled puff pastry

1 egg, lightly beaten

1 Boil, steam or microwave potato until just tender; drain. Mash in medium bowl.

2 Heat oil in small pan; cook onion, garlic and spices, stirring, until onion is soft and liquid has evaporated. Combine onion mixture in large bowl with potato and minces; mix well.

3 Preheat oven to 220°C/200°C fan-forced.

4 Cut each pastry sheet in half; divide the mince mixture among pastry halves. Shape mince mixture down one long side of pastry; brush around edges with egg, roll to enclose filling. Cut rolls in half; brush with egg, score top of each roll with sharp knife. Place rolls, seam-side down, on oiled oven trays. (Can be made ahead to this stage. Cover; refrigerate overnight or freeze.)

5 Bake, uncovered, about 25 minutes or until browned.
   PER SAUSAGE ROLL *15.7g fat; 1108kJ (265 cal)*

minted beef and pine nut pastries

preparation time 30 minutes cooking time 20 minutes makes 15

2 teaspoons olive oil

1 small brown onion (80g), finely chopped

2 cloves garlic, crushed

1 teaspoon ground cumin

1 teaspoon ground coriander

300g beef mince

2 tablespoons finely chopped fresh mint

2 tablespoons pine nuts

2 medium potatoes (400g), coarsely chopped

½ cup (60g) grated tasty cheddar cheese

10 sheets fillo pastry

125g butter, melted

TOMATO SAUCE

2 teaspoons olive oil

1 small brown onion (80g), finely chopped

2 cloves garlic, crushed

425g can crushed tomatoes

1 tablespoon tomato paste

2 teaspoons brown sugar

2 tablespoons finely chopped fresh mint

1 Heat oil in pan, add onion, garlic and spices; cook, stirring, until onion is soft. Add beef, mint and nuts; cook, stirring, until beef is browned.

2 Boil, steam or microwave potatoes until soft. Mash until smooth; add cheese, mix well. Combine beef mixture and potatoes in bowl; mix well.

3 Preheat oven to 200°C/180°C fan-forced.

4 To prevent pastry from drying out, cover with baking paper then a damp tea towel. Layer two sheets of pastry together, brushing each with butter. Cut layered sheets into three strips lengthways. Place a slightly rounded tablespoon of mixture in a corner of one strip, leaving a 1cm border. Fold corner with filling over, maintaining triangular shape; continue folding to end of fillo, retaining triangular shape. Repeat with remaining pastry, butter and beef mixture.

5 Place triangles on greased oven trays, seam-side down; brush with more butter. Bake about 8 minutes or until browned. Serve with tomato sauce.
   TOMATO SAUCE Heat oil in pan, add onion and garlic; cook, stirring, until onion is soft. Add undrained tomatoes, paste, sugar and mint; simmer, uncovered, about 5 minutes or until slightly thickened.
   PER PASTRY *12.5g fat; 786kJ (188 cal)*

chicken and prosciutto cannelloni

preparation time 30 minutes cooking time 1 hour 10 minutes serves 8

50g butter

¼ cup (35g) plain flour

⅔ cup (160ml) milk

1½ cups (375ml) chicken stock

½ cup (40g) finely grated parmesan cheese

400g fontina cheese, coarsely grated

1 tablespoon olive oil

2 medium brown onions (300g), finely chopped

3 cloves garlic, crushed

1kg chicken mince

2 tablespoons finely chopped fresh sage

850g can crushed tomatoes

½ cup (125ml) dry white wine

¼ cup (70g) tomato paste

3 teaspoons white sugar

12 fresh lasagne sheets

24 slices prosciutto (360g)

1 Heat butter in medium saucepan, add flour; cook, stirring, until mixture thickens and bubbles. Gradually stir in milk and stock; cook, stirring, until sauce boils and thickens. Remove from heat; stir in parmesan and a quarter of the fontina.

2 Heat oil in large saucepan; cook onion and garlic, stirring, until onion is soft. Add chicken; cook, stirring, until browned. Stir in sage. Combine chicken and cheese sauce in large bowl; cool.

3 Combine undrained tomatoes, wine, paste and sugar in same large pan; cook, stirring, 10 minutes. Cool 10 minutes; blend or process, in batches, until smooth.

4 Cut pasta sheets and prosciutto slices in half crossways. Place two pieces of prosciutto on each piece of pasta. Top each with ¼ cup chicken mixture; roll to enclose filling. Repeat process with remaining pasta, prosciutto and chicken mixture.

5 Preheat oven to 180°C/160°C fan-forced.

6 Oil two 3-litre (12-cup) ovenproof dishes. Pour a quarter of the tomato sauce into base of each dish; place half of the pasta rolls, seam-side down, in each dish. Pour remaining tomato sauce over rolls; sprinkle each dish with remaining fontina. (Can be made two days ahead to this stage and refrigerated, covered, or frozen for up to two months.)

7 Bake cannelloni, covered, 30 minutes. Uncover, bake further 15 minutes or until cheese melts and browns. Serve with a green salad, if desired.
PER SERVING *40.3g fat; 2998kJ (717 cal)*

TIP Pancetta or double-smoked ham can be substituted for the prosciutto.

ITALIAN

spaghetti bolognese

preparation time 15 minutes cooking time 2 hours 15 minutes serves 4

2 tablespoons olive oil

1 large brown onion (200g), finely chopped

750g beef mince

425g can crushed tomatoes

1 teaspoon finely chopped fresh basil

1 teaspoon finely chopped fresh oregano

½ teaspoon finely chopped fresh thyme

⅓ cup (95g) tomato paste

1 litre (4 cups) water

250g spaghetti

½ cup finely grated parmesan cheese

1 Heat oil in large saucepan; cook onion until golden brown. Add beef; cook until beef browns, mashing with fork occasionally to break up lumps. Pour off any surplus fat.

2 Push undrained tomatoes through sieve; add liquid to pan, discard solids. Add herbs, paste and the water; bring to a boil. Reduce heat; simmer, gently, uncovered, about 1½ hours or until nearly all liquid evaporates. (Can be made two days ahead to this stage and refrigerated, covered, or frozen for up to three months.)

3 Meanwhile, cook spaghetti in large saucepan of boiling water until just tender; drain.

4 Divide spaghetti among serving bowls; top with sauce. Serve sprinkled with cheese.
   PER SERVING *28.7g fat; 1867kJ (447 cal)*

TIP A true bolognese sauce contains no garlic, however two crushed cloves of garlic can be added to the tomatoes in step 2, if desired.

spicy lamb pizzas

preparation time 50 minutes (plus standing time) cooking time 30 minutes makes 18

1 teaspoon dried yeast

½ teaspoon white sugar

⅔ cup (160ml) warm water

1½ cups (225g) plain flour

½ teaspoon salt

¼ cup (60ml) olive oil

2 tablespoons pine nuts, roasted

1 tablespoon coarsely chopped
fresh coriander

LAMB TOPPING

2 teaspoons olive oil

250g lamb mince

1 small brown onion (80g), finely chopped

1 clove garlic, crushed

½ teaspoon ground cinnamon

1 teaspoon ground cumin

½ teaspoon sambal oelek

1 small zucchini (90g), grated

2 tablespoons tomato paste

1 large tomato (250g), finely chopped

1 Combine yeast, sugar and ¼ cup (60ml) of the water in small bowl; cover, stand in warm place about 20 minutes or until mixture is frothy.

2 Sift flour and salt into bowl. Stir in remaining water, yeast mixture and oil; mix to a soft dough. Knead dough on floured surface about 5 minutes or until smooth and elastic.

3 Place dough in oiled bowl; cover, stand in warm place about 1 hour or until dough is doubled in size. Turn dough onto lightly floured surface, knead until smooth. Divide dough into 18 pieces, roll each piece into a 10cm round.

4 Preheat oven to 200°C/180°C fan-forced.

5 Place rounds onto greased oven trays; top each with a tablespoon of lamb topping, leaving a 1cm border. Sprinkle with nuts; brush edges with a little extra oil. Bake about 15 minutes or until cooked and browned lightly. Sprinkle with coriander.

LAMB TOPPING Heat oil in pan, add lamb; cook, stirring, until browned, remove from pan. Add onion, garlic, spices, sambal oelek and zucchini to same pan; cook, stirring, until onion is soft. Return lamb to pan, add paste and tomato; cook, stirring, about 5 minutes or until thickened slightly; cool.
PER PIZZA 5.8g fat; 477kJ (114 cal)

spinach and chicken lasagne

preparation time 40 minutes cooking time 2 hours serves 4

2 teaspoons olive oil

1 medium brown onion (150g), coarsely chopped

1 clove garlic, crushed

1kg chicken mince

2 x 415g cans diced tomatoes

2 tablespoons tomato paste

1 teaspoon dried oregano

1 teaspoon dried basil

500g spinach

60g butter

¼ cup (35g) plain flour

2 cups (500ml) milk

1 cup (125g) coarsely grated cheddar cheese

175g instant lasagne sheets

1 Heat oil in large pan; cook onion and garlic, stirring, until onion is soft. Add chicken; cook, stirring, until chicken is changed in colour. Stir in undrained tomatoes, paste, oregano and basil; simmer, uncovered, stirring occasionally, about 30 minutes or until most of the liquid is absorbed.

2 Meanwhile, trim spinach; discard stems. Boil, steam or microwave spinach until just wilted; drain. Squeeze excess liquid from spinach; chop coarsely.

3 Melt butter in small pan. Add flour; cook, stirring, until mixture thickens and bubbles. Gradually stir in milk; stir until mixture boils and thickens. Remove from heat; stir in cheese and spinach.

4 Preheat oven to 180°C/160°C fan-forced.

5 Place a third of the lasagne sheets over base of oiled shallow 2-litre (8-cup capacity) ovenproof dish. Cover with half the chicken mixture, top with a third of the spinach mixture, repeat with another third of the lasagne sheets, remaining chicken mixture and a third of spinach mixture. Top with remaining lasagne sheets and spinach mixture. (Can be made ahead to this stage. Cover; refrigerate overnight or freeze.)

6 Cover lasagne with foil; bake 40 minutes. Remove foil; bake about 30 minutes or until browned lightly.

PER SERVING 51.7g fat; 4109kJ (983 cal)

minced beef and cracked wheat lasagne

preparation time 20 minutes (plus standing time) cooking time 1 hour 30 minutes serves 4

Cracked wheat is the whole unprocessed wheat berry broken into fragments. We used a medium grind in this recipe.

1 tablespoon olive oil

1 large brown onion (200g), coarsely chopped

2 cloves garlic, crushed

300g beef mince

2 x 415g cans crushed tomatoes

¼ cup (60ml) tomato paste

¼ teaspoon mixed dried herbs

3 cups (750ml) water

1 cup (160g) cracked wheat

½ teaspoon ground nutmeg

250g instant lasagne sheets

2½ cups (310g) coarsely grated cheddar cheese

1 Heat oil in large pan; cook onion and garlic, stirring, until onion is soft. Add beef; cook, stirring, until browned. Add undrained tomatoes, paste, herbs, the water and wheat; simmer, uncovered, stirring occasionally, about 25 minutes or until wheat is tender. Stir in nutmeg.

2 Preheat oven to 180°C/160°C fan-forced.

3 Spread a third of the beef mixture over base of oiled shallow 2.5-litre (10-cup capacity) ovenproof dish; cover with a third of the lasagne sheets and ¼ cup of the cheese. Repeat layering with another third of the beef mixture, another third of lasagne sheets and another ¼ cup cheese. Finish layering using remaining beef mixture, lasagne sheets and cheese.

4 Cover with foil; bake 45 minutes. (Can be made ahead to this stage. Cover; refrigerate up to two days or freeze.) Remove foil; bake, uncovered, about 15 minutes or until browned on top. Stand 10 minutes before serving.

PER SERVING 37.9g fat; 3699kJ (885 cal)

meatballs, ratatouille and ricotta rice cake

preparation time 40 minutes cooking time 1 hour 15 minutes serves 4

500g beef mince

1 small brown onion (80g), finely chopped

2 cloves garlic, crushed

1 tablespoon tomato paste

1 teaspoon ground coriander

½ cup (35g) stale breadcrumbs

½ teaspoon finely grated lemon rind

2 tablespoons olive oil

RATATOUILLE

2 tablespoons olive oil

1 large brown onion (200g), thickly sliced

2 cloves garlic, crushed

1 medium green capsicum (200g), coarsely chopped

1 medium zucchini (120g), coarsely chopped

1 finger eggplant (80g), coarsely chopped

2 tablespoons tomato paste

400g can crushed tomatoes

½ cup (125ml) vegetable stock

RICOTTA RICE CAKE

1 tablespoon polenta

2 cups (400g) ricotta cheese

¼ cup (20g) finely grated parmesan cheese

½ cup (110g) cooked long-grain rice

1 egg, separated

1 tablespoon finely shredded fresh basil

1   Combine beef, onion, garlic, paste, coriander, breadcrumbs and rind in large bowl; mix well. Using floured hands, roll level tablespoons of beef mixture into balls; place on tray. (Can be made ahead to this stage. Cover; refrigerate overnight or freeze.)

2   Heat oil in large pan; cook meatballs, in batches, until browned all over and cooked through. Drain on absorbent paper. Serve meatballs with ratatouille and ricotta rice cake.

RATATOUILLE   Heat oil in large pan; cook onion and garlic, stirring, until onion is soft. Add capsicum, zucchini and eggplant; cook, stirring, until vegetables are soft. Add paste, undrained tomatoes and stock; simmer, uncovered, about 10 minutes or until sauce thickens.

RICOTTA RICE CAKE   Preheat oven to 200°C/180°C fan-forced. Oil base of 20cm-round sandwich cake pan; line base with foil, grease foil. Sprinkle polenta over base and side of prepared pan. Combine ricotta, parmesan, rice, egg yolk and basil in large bowl; mix well. Whisk egg white in small bowl until soft peaks form; fold egg white through cheese mixture. Spread into prepared pan; bake, uncovered, about 30 minutes or until firm. Cool 5 minutes before cutting into wedges.

PER SERVING   42.2g fat; 2884kJ (690 cal)

lasagne

preparation time 40 minutes cooking time 2 hours 10 minutes serves 6

1 tablespoon olive oil

1 medium brown onion (150g), finely chopped

1 medium carrot (120g), finely chopped

1 trimmed celery stick (75g), finely chopped

2 cloves garlic, crushed

500g beef mince

⅓ cup (80ml) dry red wine

850g can crushed tomatoes

2 tablespoons tomato paste

½ cup (125ml) water

4 slices prosciutto (60g), finely chopped

1 tablespoon coarsely chopped fresh oregano

2 tablespoons coarsely chopped fresh parsley

18 instant lasagne sheets

½ cup (40g) grated parmesan cheese

CHEESE SAUCE

60g butter

⅓ cup (50g) plain flour

1 litre (4 cups) milk

¾ cup (60g) grated parmesan cheese

pinch ground nutmeg

1 Heat oil in large frying pan; cook onion, carrot, celery and garlic, stirring, until onion is soft. Add beef; cook, stirring, until browned. Add wine; bring to a boil. Stir in undrained tomatoes, paste and the water; reduce heat. Simmer, uncovered, about 1 hour or until mixture is thick. Stir in prosciutto and herbs; cool slightly.

2 Preheat oven to 180°C/160°C fan-forced.

3 Place six lasagne sheets into greased shallow 3-litre (12-cup) ovenproof dish. Spread with half of the meat sauce; drizzle with 1 cup of the cheese sauce. Repeat layers.

4 Top with remaining pasta sheets. Spread with remaining cheese sauce; sprinkle with parmesan. Bake about 45 minutes or until pasta is tender and cheese is browned lightly.

CHEESE SAUCE Heat butter in large saucepan; cook flour, stirring over heat until mixture bubbles and thickens. Remove from heat; gradually stir in milk. Cook until mixture boils and thickens; remove from heat, stir in cheese and nutmeg. Cool 10 minutes.

PER SERVING 32.4g fat; 2934kJ (702 cal)

TIP Recipe is best made a day ahead; can be made three days ahead and refrigerated, covered, or frozen for up to two months.

spicy beef pizza

preparation time 20 minutes cooking time 35 minutes serves 2

2 teaspoons olive oil

250g beef mince

1 small brown onion (80g), thinly sliced

1 clove garlic, crushed

1 teaspoon ground cumin

½ teaspoon ground coriander

½ teaspoon sweet paprika

pinch ground cinnamon

1 small carrot (70g), coarsely grated

1 small zucchini (90g), coarsely grated

½ x 400g can crushed tomatoes

2 tablespoons tomato paste

1 tablespoon coarsely chopped
fresh coriander

26cm packaged pizza base

1 tablespoon pine nuts, roasted

YOGURT TOPPING

½ cup (125ml) yogurt

1 tablespoon coarsely chopped
fresh coriander

½ teaspoon ground cumin

1 teaspoon honey

1 teaspoon lemon juice

1   Preheat oven to 200°C/180°C fan-forced.
2   Heat oil in medium pan, add beef; cook, stirring, until browned. Add onion, garlic and spices; cook, stirring, until onion is soft. Stir in carrot, zucchini, undrained tomatoes, paste and coriander. Simmer, covered, until thick, stirring occasionally; cool slightly.
3   Place pizza base on oven tray; top with beef mixture. Bake, in oven, about 15 minutes or until browned. Top pizza with yogurt topping; sprinkle with pine nuts and extra coriander, if desired.
   YOGURT TOPPING Combine ingredients in small bowl; mix well.
   PER SERVING 27.5g fat; 3779kJ (904 cal)

bolognese jaffles

preparation time 15 minutes cooking time 30 minutes makes 6

1 tablespoon olive oil

1 medium brown onion (150g),
coarsely chopped

1 clove garlic, crushed

250g beef mince

½ x 400g can crushed tomatoes

2 tablespoons tomato paste

1 beef stock cube

½ teaspoon white sugar

1 tablespoon finely chopped
fresh basil

12 slices white bread

20g butter

1   Heat oil in medium pan, add onion, garlic and beef; cook, stirring, until beef is well browned. Add undrained tomatoes, paste, crumbled stock cube and sugar to pan; simmer, uncovered, about 10 minutes or until mixture is thick. Stir in basil.

2   Spread bread on one side with butter; spoon beef mixture onto unbuttered side of six bread slices. Top with remaining bread slices, buttered-side up. Place sandwiches in jaffle iron or sandwich maker; cook until browned both sides and heated through.
   PER JAFFLE 10.2g fat; 1087kJ (260 cal)

mince and macaroni casserole

preparation time 20 minutes cooking time 30 minutes serves 4

250g macaroni pasta

1.5 litres (6 cups) boiling water

30g butter

2 medium brown onions (300g),
finely chopped

3 cloves garlic, crushed

500g beef mince

⅓ cup (50g) plain flour

2 tablespoons tomato paste

1 teaspoon mild English mustard

3 cups (750ml) milk

1 cup (125g) coarsely grated cheddar cheese

1 cup (100g) coarsely grated mozzarella cheese

¼ cup coarsely chopped fresh flat-leaf parsley

1   Spread pasta over base of 3-litre (12-cup) deep microwave-safe dish, cover with the boiling water; cook, uncovered, on HIGH (100%) about 10 minutes or until just tender, stirring twice during cooking. Drain pasta, cover to keep warm.

2   Combine butter, onion and garlic in same dish; cook, uncovered, on HIGH (100%) 5 minutes. Stir in beef; cook, uncovered, on HIGH (100%) 10 minutes, stirring twice during cooking. Stir in flour, paste and mustard; cook, uncovered, on HIGH (100%) 2 minutes. Stir in milk; cook, uncovered, on HIGH (100%) about 6 minutes or until mixture boils and thickens, stirring twice during cooking.

3   Stir in pasta and half the combined cheeses and parsley. Top with remaining cheese and parsley mixture; cook, uncovered, on HIGH (100%) about 2 minutes or until cheese melts.
   PER SERVING 39.2g fat; 3566kJ (835 cal)

fettuccine with meatballs in rosemary paprika sauce

preparation time 15 minutes cooking time 45 minutes serves 2

250g lean beef mince

½ cup (35g) stale breadcrumbs

1 tablespoon finely chopped fresh
 flat-leaf parsley

1 tablespoon finely chopped fresh chives

1 egg white

1 teaspoon Worcestershire sauce

2 teaspoons olive oil

250g fettuccine

ROSEMARY PAPRIKA SAUCE

425g can crushed tomatoes

1 cup (250ml) water

2 tablespoons dry red wine

1 medium brown onion (150g), finely chopped

½ teaspoon Worcestershire sauce

1 teaspoon sweet paprika

3 sprigs rosemary

1 Combine beef, breadcrumbs, parsley, chives, egg white and sauce in large bowl. Shape mixture into small meatballs.

2 Heat oil in medium saucepan; cook meatballs until well browned all over and cooked through. Drain on absorbent paper.

3 Meanwhile, cook pasta in large saucepan of boiling water until just tender; drain.

4 Add meatballs to rosemary paprika sauce; mix well. Stir until heated through. (Can be made two days ahead to this stage and refrigerated, covered, or frozen for up to three months.)

5 Serve pasta with meatballs in rosemary paprika sauce.
   ROSEMARY PAPRIKA SAUCE Combine ingredients in medium saucepan; bring to a boil. Reduce heat; simmer, uncovered, about 20 minutes or until thickened slightly.
   PER SERVING *15.8g fat; 3303kJ (790 cal)*

beef and bean stew with polenta wedges

preparation time 15 minutes cooking time 40 minutes serves 4

2 teaspoons olive oil

1 small brown onion (80g), finely chopped

1 clove garlic, crushed

300g beef mince

2 x 420g cans soya beans, rinsed, drained

¼ cup (60ml) tomato paste

1 tablespoon Worcestershire sauce

2 teaspoons mild chilli sauce

2 tablespoons barbecue sauce

2 cups (500ml) beef stock

2 tablespoons finely chopped fresh flat-leaf parsley

⅓ cup (80ml) sour cream

POLENTA WEDGES

1 tablespoon olive oil

1 medium brown onion (150g), thinly sliced

3 cups (750ml) beef stock

1½ cups (250g) polenta

½ cup (60g) coarsely grated cheddar cheese

1 Heat oil in large pan; cook onion and garlic, stirring, until onion is soft. Add beef; cook, stirring, until browned. Stir in beans, paste, sauces and stock; simmer, uncovered, stirring occasionally, about 20 minutes or until mixture thickens. (Can be made ahead to this stage. Cover; refrigerate overnight or freeze.) Stir in parsley just before serving. Serve stew with polenta wedges and sour cream.

POLENTA WEDGES Grease a 20cm x 30cm lamington pan; line base with baking paper. Heat oil in large pan; cook onion, stirring, about 5 minutes or until just browned; remove from pan. Bring stock to a boil in the same pan. Gradually stir in polenta; simmer, stirring, about 5 minutes or until mixture thickens. Stir in cheese and reserved onion. Press polenta mixture into prepared pan, cover; refrigerate until firm. (Can be made ahead to this stage. Cover; refrigerate overnight or freeze.)

PER SERVING 27.9g fat; 3076kJ (736 cal)

rigatoni bolognese

preparation time 5 minutes cooking time 30 minutes serves 4

1 medium brown onion (150g), coarsely chopped

1 small carrot (70g), coarsely chopped

1 trimmed celery stick (100g), coarsely chopped

1 tablespoon olive oil

50g butter

2 cloves garlic, crushed

2 Italian-style sausages (170g)

500g beef mince

2 tablespoons tomato paste

½ cup (125ml) dry white wine

¼ cup (60ml) beef stock

425g can crushed tomatoes

2 tablespoons finely chopped fresh basil

2 tablespoons finely chopped fresh flat-leaf parsley

500g rigatoni

¼ cup (20g) coarsely grated parmesan cheese

1 Blend or process onion, carrot and celery until chopped finely.

2 Heat oil and butter in large saucepan; cook onion mixture and garlic, stirring occasionally, 5 minutes.

3 Meanwhile, squeeze filling from sausages; discard casings. Add sausage filling and beef to pan; cook, stirring, until meats are browned lightly.

4 Stir in paste and wine; bring to a boil. Reduce heat; simmer, uncovered, 2 minutes. Add stock and undrained tomatoes; return to a boil. Reduce heat; simmer, uncovered, about 20 minutes or until bolognese thickens. Stir in herbs.

5 Meanwhile, cook pasta in large saucepan of boiling water, uncovered, until just tender; drain.

6 Serve pasta topped with bolognese and sprinkled with cheese.
PER SERVING *36.9g fat; 3933kJ (941 cal)*

spaghetti and meatballs

preparation time 15 minutes cooking time 20 minutes serves 4

500g pork mince

2 tablespoons coarsely chopped
fresh flat-leaf parsley

1 clove garlic, crushed

1 egg

1 cup (70g) stale breadcrumbs

1 tablespoon tomato paste

2 tablespoons olive oil

400g can crushed tomatoes

600ml bottled tomato pasta sauce

375g spaghetti

⅓ cup (25g) finely grated romano cheese

1 Combine pork, parsley, garlic, egg, breadcrumbs and paste in large bowl; roll tablespoons of pork mixture into balls. Heat oil in large saucepan; cook meatballs, in batches, until browned all over.

2 Place undrained tomatoes and sauce in same pan; bring to a boil. Return meatballs to pan, reduce heat; simmer, uncovered, about 10 minutes or until meatballs are cooked through.

3 Meanwhile, cook pasta in large saucepan of boiling water, uncovered, until just tender; drain. Divide pasta among serving bowls; top with meatballs, sprinkle with cheese.
PER SERVING *23g fat; 3149kJ (753 cal)*

TIPS Meatballs can be made and fried a day ahead; keep, covered, in the refrigerator until the sauce is made.
To save time when making the recipe on another occasion, double the meatball quantities and freeze half of them after frying. Thaw meatballs overnight in refrigerator before adding to the sauce.

frypan pizza

preparation time 25 minutes cooking time 40 minutes serves 4

1½ cups (225g) self-raising flour

30g butter

½ cup (125ml) milk, approximately

60g button mushrooms, sliced

½ medium green capsicum (100g), finely chopped

½ medium red capsicum (100g), finely chopped

1½ cups (185g) grated cheddar cheese

½ teaspoon sweet paprika

MINCE TOPPING

1 tablespoon olive oil

1 small brown onion (80g), finely chopped

1 clove garlic, crushed

250g beef mince

400g can crushed tomatoes

2 tablespoons tomato paste

½ small beef stock cube

½ teaspoon white sugar

¼ teaspoon dried oregano leaves

1 Sift flour into large bowl, rub in butter; add enough milk to mix to a soft dough. Knead dough on floured surface until smooth.

2 Press dough evenly into 23cm frying pan; spread with mince topping, sprinkle with mushrooms, capsicums and cheese.

3 Cover pan, cook over medium heat about 20 minutes or until pizza is browned underneath and cooked through. Sprinkle with paprika.
   MINCE TOPPING Heat oil in pan, add onion and garlic; cook, stirring, until onion is soft. Add beef; cook, stirring, until beef is browned. Add undrained tomatoes and remaining ingredients; simmer, uncovered, until thick. Allow to cool.
   PER SERVING *33g fat; 2658kJ (636 cal)*

savoury mince with fresh herbs

preparation time 20 minutes cooking time 40 minutes serves 4

1 tablespoon olive oil

2 medium brown onions (300g), coarsely chopped

1 large carrot (180g), coarsely chopped

3 cloves garlic, crushed

1kg beef mince

4 medium zucchini (480g), coarsely chopped

400g can crushed tomatoes

⅔ cup (160ml) tomato paste

2 tablespoons Worcestershire sauce

2 beef stock cubes

2 tablespoons fruit chutney

¼ cup coarsely chopped fresh oregano

2 tablespoons coarsely chopped fresh basil

1 tablespoon coarsely chopped fresh flat-leaf parsley

1 cup (125g) frozen peas, thawed

1 Combine oil, onion, carrot and garlic in large microwave-safe dish; cook, covered, on HIGH (100%) 10 minutes, stirring once during cooking. Stir in beef; cook, covered, on HIGH (100%) 7 minutes, stirring once during cooking.

2 Add zucchini, undrained tomatoes, paste, sauce, crumbled stock cubes, chutney and herbs; cook, covered, on HIGH (100%) 15 minutes, stirring three times during cooking. Stir in peas; cook, covered, on HIGH (100%) 5 minutes.
   PER SERVING *23g fat; 2349kJ (562 cal)*

meatballs with chilli mushroom sauce

preparation time 15 minutes cooking time 20 minutes serves 4

500g pork and veal mince

1 cup (70g) stale breadcrumbs

¼ cup finely chopped fresh oregano

3 cloves garlic, crushed

⅓ cup (95g) tomato paste

1 egg, lightly beaten

1 tablespoon olive oil

250g button mushrooms, thinly sliced

850g can crushed tomatoes

¼ cup (60ml) mild chilli sauce

1 Preheat oven to 200°C/180°C fan-forced.

2 Combine mince, breadcrumbs, oregano, garlic, paste and egg in medium bowl; roll level tablespoons of mixture into balls. Place meatballs on oiled oven tray; bake, uncovered, about 15 minutes or until cooked through.

3 Meanwhile, heat oil in large saucepan; cook mushrooms, stirring, until just soft. Add undrained tomatoes and sauce to pan; bring to a boil. Reduce heat; simmer, uncovered, 5 minutes. Add meatballs; cook, stirring, 2 minutes.
PER SERVING *16.4g fat; 1649kJ (394 cal)*

TIP Recipe can be made two days ahead and refrigerated, covered, or frozen for up to three months.

meatballs in tomato sauce

preparation time 20 minutes cooking time 30 minutes serves 4

500g beef mince

8 green onions, finely chopped

1 clove garlic, crushed

1 tablespoon tomato paste

½ cup (35g) stale breadcrumbs

2 tablespoons finely chopped fresh flat-leaf parsley

1 egg

⅓ cup (50g) plain flour

400g can crushed tomatoes

½ teaspoon chilli powder

1 teaspoon Worcestershire sauce

2 tablespoons dry white wine

1 Using hands, combine beef, half the onion, garlic, paste, breadcrumbs, parsley and egg in large bowl; shape into eight meatballs. Toss meatballs in flour, shake off excess. Place meatballs around edge of large shallow microwave-safe dish.

2 Combine undrained tomatoes and remaining ingredients in bowl; pour over meatballs in dish. Cook, covered, on MEDIUM (55%) 20 minutes. Uncover; cook on MEDIUM (55%) 10 minutes.
PER SERVING *10.6g fat, 1187kJ (284 cal)*

chicken stir-fry noodles

preparation time 10 minutes cooking time 20 minutes serves 4

250g dried thin rice noodles

1 tablespoon peanut oil

3 eggs, lightly beaten

1 medium brown onion (150g), finely chopped

2 cloves garlic, crushed

2 tablespoons grated fresh ginger

500g chicken mince

500g baby buk choy, coarsely chopped

¼ cup (60ml) light soy sauce

½ cup coarsely chopped fresh coriander

3 cups (240g) bean sprouts

1 Place noodles in large heatproof bowl; cover with boiling water. Stand until just tender; drain.

2 Brush heated wok with a little of the oil. Add half the egg; swirl to cover base of wok. Cook, covered, about 3 minutes or until cooked through. Remove omelette from wok; repeat with remaining egg. Roll omelettes tightly; slice thinly.

3 Heat remaining oil in wok; stir-fry onion, garlic and ginger until onion softens. Add chicken; stir-fry until chicken is cooked through.

4 Add buk choy, sauce and coriander; stir-fry until buk choy is just tender. Stir in noodles and sprouts; serve immediately, topped with omelette.
PER SERVING *19.8g fat; 2149kJ (514 cal)*

TIPS Create a vegetarian version of this dish by substituting fried tofu for the chicken.
You can substitute choy sum, chinese broccoli or trimmed, thinly sliced buk choy for the baby buk choy.

ASIAN FLAVOURS

nepalese pork mince curry

preparation time 15 minutes **cooking time** 20 minutes **serves** 4

2 tablespoons peanut oil

2 tablespoons yellow mustard seeds

2 teaspoons ground cumin

1 teaspoon ground turmeric

2 teaspoons garam masala

3 cloves garlic, crushed

4cm piece fresh ginger (20g), grated

2 medium brown onions (300g), finely chopped

800g pork mince

½ cup (125ml) water

¼ cup coarsely chopped fresh coriander

1 Heat oil in large frying pan; cook seeds, stirring, about 2 minutes or until seeds pop. Add cumin, turmeric and garam masala; cook, stirring, 2 minutes.

2 Add garlic, ginger and onion; cook, stirring, until onion softens.

3 Add pork; cook, stirring, until cooked through. Add the water; simmer, uncovered, 15 minutes. Remove from heat, stir in coriander.
PER SERVING *23.4g fat; 1655kJ (396 cal)*

pork and lemon grass stir-fry

preparation time 20 minutes **cooking time** 20 minutes **serves** 4

Palm sugar, made from the distilled sap of the sugar palm, is also known as jaggery or gula jawa and is available from Asian food stores; use brown sugar if unavailable.

1 tablespoon peanut oil

2 tablespoons finely chopped lemon grass

2 fresh small red thai chillies, finely chopped

2cm piece fresh galangal (35g), finely chopped

2 cloves garlic, crushed

500g pork mince

1 tablespoon thai-style red curry paste

100g green beans, coarsely chopped

1½ tablespoons fish sauce

2 tablespoons lime juice

1 tablespoon grated palm sugar

1 small red onion (100g), thinly sliced

2 green onions, thinly sliced

¼ cup firmly packed thai basil leaves

½ cup firmly packed fresh coriander leaves

¼ cup (75g) roasted peanuts, coarsely chopped

4 iceberg lettuce leaves

1 Heat oil in wok; cook lemon grass, chilli, galangal and garlic, stirring, until fragrant. Add pork; cook, stirring, until cooked through. Add curry paste; cook, stirring, until fragrant.

2 Add beans, sauce, juice and sugar to wok; cook, stirring, about 5 minutes or until beans are just tender. Remove from heat.

3 Add onions, basil, coriander and half of the peanuts to pork mixture; stir to combine.

4 Serve pork mixture in lettuce cups sprinkled with remaining peanuts.
   PER SERVING *25.2g fat; 1638kJ (391 cal)*

pork and prawn with crispy fried noodles

preparation time 25 minutes (plus standing time) cooking time 30 minutes serves 4

300g fresh silken firm tofu

vegetable oil, for deep-frying

60g rice vermicelli

2 tablespoons peanut oil

2 eggs, lightly beaten

1 tablespoon water

2 cloves garlic, crushed

2 fresh small red thai chillies, finely chopped

1 small green chilli, finely chopped

2 tablespoons grated palm sugar

2 tablespoons fish sauce

2 tablespoons tomato sauce

1 tablespoon rice wine vinegar

200g pork mince

200g small shelled cooked prawns, coarsely chopped

6 green onions, thinly sliced

¼ cup firmly packed fresh coriander leaves

1 Pat tofu all over with absorbent paper; cut into slices, then cut each slice into 1cm-wide matchsticks. Spread tofu on tray lined with absorbent paper; cover tofu with more absorbent paper, stand at least 20 minutes.

2 Meanwhile, heat vegetable oil in wok; deep-fry vermicelli quickly, in batches, until puffed. Drain on absorbent paper.

3 Using same heated oil, deep-fry drained tofu, in batches, until lightly browned. Drain on absorbent paper. Cool oil; remove from wok and reserve for another use.

4 Heat 2 teaspoons of the peanut oil in same cleaned wok; add half the combined egg and water, swirl wok to make thin omelette. Cook, uncovered, until egg is just set. Remove from wok; roll omelette, cut into thin strips. Heat another 2 teaspoons of the peanut oil in same wok; repeat process with remaining egg mixture.

5 Combine garlic, chillies, sugar, sauces and vinegar in small bowl; pour half of the chilli mixture into small jug, reserve.

6 Combine pork in bowl with remaining chilli mixture. Heat remaining peanut oil in same wok; stir-fry pork mixture about 5 minutes or until pork is cooked through. Add prawns; stir fry 1 minute. Add tofu; stir-fry, tossing gently to combine.

7 Remove wok from heat, add reserved chilli mixture and half the onion, toss to combine. Add vermicelli; toss gently to combine. Sprinkle with remaining onion, omelette strips and coriander.

PER SERVING 25.8g fat; 1770kJ (423 cal)

kofta curry

preparation time 35 minutes (plus refrigeration time) cooking time 1 hour serves 4

800g chicken mince

2cm piece fresh ginger (10g), grated

½ teaspoon ground cinnamon

⅓ cup coarsely chopped fresh coriander

4 cloves garlic, crushed

2 tablespoons ghee

1 medium brown onion (150g), finely chopped

2 fresh long red chillies, finely chopped

2 teaspoons ground coriander

1 teaspoon ground cumin

½ teaspoon ground turmeric

1 teaspoon ground fenugreek

1 teaspoon garam masala

4 medium tomatoes (600g), peeled, coarsely chopped

2 cups (500ml) chicken stock

½ cup firmly packed fresh coriander leaves

1 Combine chicken, ginger, cinnamon, chopped coriander and half the garlic in medium bowl; roll level tablespoons of the mixture into balls. Place balls on tray, cover; refrigerate kofta for 30 minutes.

2 Meanwhile, heat one tablespoon of the ghee in large saucepan; cook onion, chilli, spices and remaining garlic, stirring, until onion is browned lightly. Add tomato; cook, stirring, about 5 minutes or until tomato softens. Add stock; simmer, uncovered, about 15 minutes or until sauce thickens slightly.

3 Heat remaining ghee in medium frying pan; cook kofta, in batches, until browned. Add kofta to sauce; simmer, uncovered, about 10 minutes or until kofta are cooked through. Stir in coriander leaves off the heat. Serve with a cucumber raita, if desired.

PER SERVING 25.7g fat; 1797kJ (430 cal)

gyoza with soy vinegar sauce

preparation time 40 minutes (plus refrigeration time) cooking time 15 minutes makes 40

300g pork mince

2 tablespoons kecap manis

1 teaspoon white sugar

1 tablespoon sake

1 egg, lightly beaten

2 teaspoons sesame oil

3 cups (240g) finely shredded wombok

4 green onions, thinly sliced

40 gyoza or gow gee wrappers

1 tablespoon vegetable oil

SOY VINEGAR SAUCE

½ cup (125ml) light soy sauce

¼ cup (60ml) red wine vinegar

2 tablespoons white vinegar

2 tablespoons sweet chilli sauce

1 Combine pork, kecap manis, sugar, sake, egg, sesame oil, wombok and onion in medium bowl; refrigerate 1 hour.

2 Place a heaped teaspoon of the pork mixture in centre of one wrapper; brush wrapper along one side of pork mixture with a little water. Pleat damp side of wrapper only; pinch both sides of wrapper together to seal. Repeat with remaining pork mixture and wrappers.

3 Cover base of large frying pan with water; bring to a boil. Add dumplings, in batches, reduce heat. Simmer, covered, 3 minutes; using slotted spoon, remove dumplings from pan. Drain and dry pan.

4 Heat vegetable oil in same pan; cook dumplings, in batches, unpleated side and base only, until golden brown.

5 Serve hot with soy vinegar sauce.
   SOY VINEGAR SAUCE Combine ingredients in small bowl.
   PER GYOZA 1.4g fat, 139kJ (31 cal)
   PER TABLESPOON SAUCE 0.1g fat; 35kJ (8 cal)

TIP The gyoza filling can be prepared four hours ahead and refrigerated, covered.

beef kofta

preparation time 30 minutes (plus refrigeration time) cooking time 55 minutes serves 6

750g beef mince

2 tablespoons finely chopped fresh mint

2 teaspoons finely grated fresh ginger

1 teaspoon ground coriander

½ teaspoon garam masala

1 teaspoon chilli powder

¼ cup (60ml) yogurt

3 tablespoons ghee

2 medium brown onions (300g), thinly sliced

2 cloves garlic, crushed

½ teaspoon ground cardamom

1 teaspoon garam masala, extra

1 teaspoon ground turmeric

1 teaspoon cumin seeds

2 medium tomatoes (380g), coarsely chopped

1 tablespoon tomato paste

2 baby eggplants (120g), coarsely chopped

2 fresh small red thai chillies, chopped finely

1 cup (250ml) beef stock

1 tablespoon coarsely chopped fresh coriander

1 Combine beef, mint, ginger, ground coriander, garam masala, chilli powder and yogurt in medium bowl. Mould tablespoons of mince mixture into oval kofta shapes, place on tray; cover, refrigerate 1 hour.

2 Heat half the ghee in large frying pan; cook kofta, in batches, until browned all over. Drain on absorbent paper.

3 Heat remaining ghee in same pan; cook onions, garlic, cardamom, extra garam masala, turmeric and cumin, stirring, until onions are browned lightly.

4 Add tomatoes, paste, eggplants and chillies; cook, stirring, 5 minutes or until vegetables are soft.

5 Add stock and kofta; simmer, covered, 20 minutes. Simmer, uncovered, 10 minutes or until kofta are cooked through and sauce is thickened. Just before serving, stir in chopped coriander.

PER SERVING *15g fat; 1150kJ (275 cal)*

ASIAN FLAVOURS

singapore noodles

preparation time 15 minutes cooking time 10 minutes serves 4

250g dried thin egg noodles

2 tablespoons peanut oil

4 eggs, lightly beaten

1 tablespoon water

1 medium brown onion (150g),
finely chopped

2 cloves garlic, crushed

2 tablespoons mild curry paste

200g pork mince

200g chinese barbecued pork, thinly sliced

200g shelled cooked small prawns

3 green onions, coarsely chopped

¼ cup (60ml) salt-reduced soy sauce

2 tablespoons oyster sauce

2 fresh small red thai chillies, finely chopped

1   Cook noodles in large saucepan of boiling water, uncovered, until
just tender; drain.

2   Meanwhile, heat 2 teaspoons of the oil in wok; add half the combined
eggs and water, swirl wok to make thin omelette. Cook, uncovered,
until egg is just set. Remove from wok; roll omelette, cut into thin
strips. Heat another 2 teaspoons of the oil in wok; repeat process with
remaining egg mixture.

3   Heat remaining oil in wok; stir-fry brown onion and garlic until onion
softens. Add paste; stir fry until fragrant. Add pork mince; stir-fry until
changed in colour. Add barbecued pork, prawns, green onion, sauces,
chilli and half the omelette; stir-fry until heated through. Add noodles;
toss gently to combine, serve topped with remaining omelette.
PER SERVING *24.5g fat; 2683kJ (642 cal)*

savoury pancake *okonomi-yaki*

preparation time 10 minutes (plus standing time) **cooking time** 10 minutes **serves** 4

Okonomi means "your choice" since these pancakes are usually prepared to order with a choice of fillings so each diner can suit his or her taste. It's important not to leave the batter standing too long or it will become sticky. Ao-nori is made from laver seaweed, which grows on rocks in bays and at the mouths of rivers. It is sold dried in flakes for sprinkling as a garnish. Beni-shoga is finely sliced or shredded pickled ginger, which is deep red in colour. Bonito is an oily fish which, when dried and flaked, is widely used in the Japanese kitchen.

2 cups (300g) plain flour

1½ teaspoons baking powder

1½ cups (375ml) secondary dashi

1 egg, lightly beaten

2 large cabbage leaves

125g pork mince

2 tablespoons vegetable oil

½ cup (125ml) Japanese Worcestershire sauce

2 tablespoons red pickled ginger (beni-shoga)

1 tablespoon shredded dried seaweed (ao-nori)

¼ cup (3g) smoked dried bonito flakes (katsuobushi)

1 Sift flour and baking powder together in medium bowl. Gradually add combined dashi and egg, mixing quickly until smooth; do not overmix. Cover; stand 30 minutes.

2 Remove thick ribs from cabbage leaves and discard; slice remaining leaves thinly. Add cabbage and pork to batter; mix gently.

3 Heat a quarter of the oil in medium frying pan over low heat. Spoon in a quarter of the batter and flatten with a spatula. When bubbles begin to appear in mixture, turn over and brush cooked side with sauce. Turn pancake over again and brush other side with sauce. Quickly repeat once more, so the sauce caramelises onto the pancake. Remove from pan, cover; keep warm. Repeat with remaining oil and batter.

4 Serve pancakes sprinkled with pickled ginger, seaweed and bonito flakes.
PER SERVING *20.1g fat; 2328kJ (557 cal)*

TIPS Japanese Worcestershire sauce comes in different strengths; most are milder than western Worcestershire so adjust the amount added according to taste.
Okonomi-yaki packet mixes are available from Asian food shops, either plain or with octopus.
SERVING SUGGESTION Chopped octopus is a particular favourite in this dish in Japan.

meatballs in spicy coconut milk

preparation time 25 minutes cooking time 20 minutes serves 4

800g beef mince

2 eggs

2 teaspoons cornflour

2 cloves garlic, crushed

1 tablespoon finely chopped fresh coriander

1 fresh long red chilli, finely chopped

2 purple shallots (50g), coarsely chopped

3 cloves garlic, quartered

1 teaspoon chilli flakes

7 fresh long red chillies, coarsely chopped

2 tablespoons peanut oil

2cm piece fresh galangal (10g), thinly sliced

3 large tomatoes (660g), seeded,
coarsely chopped

400ml can coconut milk

1 tablespoon kecap asin

1 large tomato (220g), seeded, diced

½ cup (40g) fried shallots

1 fresh small red thai chilli, thinly sliced

1 Combine beef, eggs, cornflour, crushed garlic, coriander and finely chopped chilli in medium bowl; roll level tablespoons of mixture into balls. Place meatballs, in single layer, in large baking-paper-lined bamboo steamer. Steam, covered, over wok of simmering water 10 minutes.

2 Meanwhile, blend or process purple shallots, quartered garlic, chilli flakes, coarsely chopped chilli and half of the oil until mixture forms a paste.

3 Heat remaining oil in wok; cook shallot paste and galangal, stirring, about 1 minute or until fragrant. Add chopped tomato; cook, stirring, 1 minute. Add coconut milk, kecap asin and meatballs; simmer, uncovered, stirring occasionally, about 5 minutes or until meatballs are cooked through and sauce thickens slightly.

4 Serve curry topped with diced tomato, fried shallots and thinly sliced chilli.
   PER SERVING *47.1g fat; 2721kJ (651 cal)*

fried soba

preparation time 15 minutes cooking time 20 minutes serves 4

Soba are noodles made from buckwheat and wheat flours. Ao-nori is a dried laver seaweed that grows on rocks in bays and at the mouths of rivers. It is sold in flakes for sprinkling as a garnish.

250g dried soba

1 tablespoon sesame oil

2 tablespoons vegetable oil

300g pork mince

1 medium brown onion (150g),
cut into eight wedges

1 clove garlic, crushed

1 teaspoon grated fresh ginger

10 cups (500g) finely shredded cabbage

1 medium red capsicum (200g), sliced finely

2 tablespoons red pickled ginger (beni-shoga)

2 teaspoons shredded dried seaweed (ao-nori)

SAUCE

1 tablespoon white sugar

¼ cup (60ml) mirin

2 tablespoons sake

¼ cup (60ml) japanese soy sauce

1 Cook noodles in large saucepan of boiling water, uncovered, until just tender, drain.

2 Heat sesame oil and 1 tablespoon of the vegetable oil in a wok; stir-fry pork over medium heat until browned lightly. Remove from wok; cover to keep warm.

3 In same wok, heat remaining vegetable oil; stir-fry onion, garlic and fresh ginger until onion softens. Add cabbage and capsicum; cook until tender. Stir through pickled ginger, pork, noodles and sauce until hot. Serve sprinkled with seaweed.

SAUCE Heat ingredients in small saucepan, stirring, until sugar dissolves.

PER SERVING 20.1g fat; 2274kJ (544 cal)

pork, chicken and rice noodle stir-fry

preparation time 20 minutes cooking time 25 minutes serves 4

¼ cup (55g) white sugar

⅓ cup (80ml) mild chilli sauce

¼ cup (60ml) fish sauce

1 tablespoon light soy sauce

1 tablespoon tomato sauce

500g chicken breast fillets, thickly sliced

150g fresh wide rice noodles

1 tablespoon sesame oil

500g pork mince

1 large brown onion (200g), thickly sliced

2 cloves garlic, crushed

2 cups (160g) bean sprouts

1 cup coarsely chopped fresh coriander

⅓ cup (50g) coarsely chopped roasted peanuts

1 Combine sugar and sauces in large bowl. Add chicken; toss to coat in mixture.

2 Rinse noodles in strainer under hot water. Separate with fork; drain.

3 Meanwhile, drain chicken mixture; reserve marinade. Heat half the oil in wok; stir-fry chicken mixture, in batches, until chicken is browned all over and cooked through.

4 Heat remaining oil in wok; stir-fry pork, onion and garlic until pork is cooked through. Return chicken to wok with reserved marinade. Stir-fry until marinade comes to a boil; remove from heat. Add noodles, sprouts, coriander and peanuts; toss gently to combine.

PER SERVING *27.2g fat; 2707kJ (648 cal)*

spicy chicken salad in witlof

preparation time 20 minutes cooking time 15 minutes makes 24

1 tablespoon sesame oil

300g chicken mince

1 tablespoon fish sauce

2 tablespoons lime juice

1 tablespoon palm sugar

1 tablespoon finely chopped vietnamese mint

1 tablespoon finely chopped fresh coriander

4 baby witlof, separated

CORIANDER PASTE

2 coriander roots, coarsely chopped

3 cloves garlic, peeled

4cm piece fresh ginger (20g), finely grated

10 white peppercorns

1 Make coriander paste.
2 Heat oil in wok, add coriander paste; cook, stirring, until fragrant.
3 Add chicken; cook, stirring, until browned lightly. Add sauce, juice and sugar; simmer gently, uncovered, 5 minutes or until thickened slightly. Stir in mint and coriander.
4 Divide mixture evenly among witlof leaves.
CORIANDER PASTE In a small blender, spice grinder or mortar and pestle, blend or pound ingredients until finely chopped.
PER LEAF *1.8g fat; 134kJ (32 cal)*

TIP The chicken filling can be prepared several hours ahead; keep, covered, in refrigerator. Assemble just before serving.

fish ball and green peppercorn red curry

preparation time 30 minutes cooking time 15 minutes serves 4

750g firm white fish fillets, coarsely chopped

3 cloves garlic, quartered

2 tablespoons soy sauce

2 tablespoons cornflour

2 tablespoons finely chopped coriander root and stem mixture

2cm piece fresh ginger (10g), grated

2 teaspoons peanut oil

⅓ cup (100g) red curry paste

2 x 400g cans coconut milk

4 x 5cm stems pickled green peppercorns (20g), rinsed, drained

2 teaspoons grated palm sugar

2 fresh kaffir lime leaves, finely shredded

2 teaspoons fish sauce

115g baby corn, halved lengthways

1 cup bean sprouts (80g)

1 fresh long red chilli, thinly sliced

¼ cup loosely packed fresh coriander leaves

1 Blend or process fish, garlic, soy sauce, cornflour, coriander mixture and fresh ginger until mixture forms a paste; roll level tablespoons of mixture into balls.

2 Cook oil and curry paste in large saucepan, stirring, until fragrant. Gradually stir in coconut milk; simmer, uncovered, 5 minutes. Add fish balls, peppercorn stems, sugar, lime leaves, fish sauce and corn; cook, uncovered, about 5 minutes or until fish balls are cooked through.

3 Serve curry sprinkled with sprouts, chilli and coriander leaves.
PER SERVING *47.6g fat; 2972kJ (711 cal)*

TIP Keep uncooked fish balls, covered, in single layer on tray, in the refrigerator until required. The fish balls will firm up and the flavours of the mixture will blend together. You can also freeze uncooked fish balls in snap-lock plastic bags.

kashmiri lamb kofta

preparation time 25 minutes cooking time 35 minutes serves 6

2 teaspoons ground cumin

2 teaspoons ground coriander

2 teaspoons garam masala

1 teaspoon chilli powder

½ teaspoon ground turmeric

750g lamb mince

4 cloves garlic, crushed

2 teaspoons grated fresh ginger

⅔ cup (160ml) yogurt

2 tablespoons ghee

1 large brown onion (200g), finely chopped

2 tablespoons full cream milk powder

2 tablespoons ground almonds

1 teaspoon white sugar

1½ cups (375ml) hot water

⅓ cup (80ml) yogurt, extra

1 Combine spices in small bowl.

2 Combine lamb, garlic, ginger, 1 tablespoon of the yogurt and half of the spice mixture in large bowl; mix well. Using floured hands, roll tablespoons of spicy mince mixture into round kofta shapes.

3 Heat ghee in large saucepan; cook onion, stirring, until fragrant. Gradually add the remaining yogurt, milk powder, nuts, sugar and the hot water. Bring to a boil, then simmer, uncovered, 5 minutes, stirring occasionally, or until mixture thickens slightly.

4 Add kofta; simmer, covered, 10 minutes. Simmer, uncovered, 10 minutes or until kofta are cooked through and sauce is thickened. Serve topped with extra yogurt.

PER SERVING *18.2g fat; 1283kJ (307 cal)*

spicy thai-style chicken

preparation time 10 minutes cooking time 20 minutes serves 4

500g lean chicken mince

3 cloves garlic, crushed

⅓ cup (80ml) sweet chilli sauce

1 tablespoon fish sauce

2 tablespoons salt-reduced soy sauce

4 green onions, finely chopped

2 tablespoons finely shredded fresh basil

500g baby buk choy, halved

1   Cook chicken in heated oiled wok, stirring, until cooked through.
2   Add garlic and chilli sauce; cook, stirring, until mixture is browned. Stir in fish sauce, soy sauce, onion and basil.
3   Meanwhile, boil, steam or microwave buk choy until tender; drain.
4   Serve chicken immediately, with buk choy.
    PER SERVING *7.8g fat; 908kJ (217 cal)*

pan-fried dumplings *gyoza*

preparation time 20 minutes (plus refrigeration time) cooking time 10 minutes makes 50

You can vary the filling of these dumplings by adding chopped prawns, cheese, capsicum or scrambled egg. You'll need about a quarter of a medium cabbage to make this recipe.

300g pork mince

2 tablespoons japanese soy sauce

¼ teaspoon white pepper

1 teaspoon white sugar

1 tablespoon sake

1 egg, lightly beaten

2 teaspoons sesame oil

6½ cups (325g) finely chopped cabbage

4 green onions, finely chopped

50 gyoza or gow gee wrappers

1 tablespoon vegetable oil

1 Mix pork, sauce, pepper, sugar, sake, egg, sesame oil, cabbage and onion in medium bowl. Refrigerate 1 hour.
2 Take a wrapper and wet the edge of one side. Place a rounded teaspoon of pork mixture in centre of wrapper and pleat the damp side of wrapper only. Pinch both sides together to seal. Repeat with remaining wrappers and pork mixture.
3 Cover base of large frying pan with water, bring to a boil. Add dumplings, in batches; reduce heat and simmer, covered, 3 minutes. Remove dumplings from pan with slotted spoon; drain and dry pan.
4 Heat vegetable oil in same frying pan; cook dumplings, uncovered, in batches, unpleated side and base only, until golden.
PER DUMPLING *1.2g fat; 76kJ (19 cal)*

TIP Serve gyoza with soy sauce mixed with chilli oil, or rice vinegar or ponzu sauce.

combination wonton soup

preparation time 30 minutes cooking time 10 minutes serves 4

150g chicken mince

1 green onion, thinly sliced

2 tablespoons light soy sauce

16 wonton wrappers

24 uncooked medium prawns (600g)

1.5 litres (6 cups) chicken stock

100g chinese barbecued pork, thinly sliced

100g fresh shiitake mushrooms, thinly sliced

150g baby buk choy, coarsely chopped

4 green onions, thinly sliced, extra

1 Combine chicken, onion and half of the sauce in small bowl.
2 Place a heaped teaspoon of chicken mixture in centre of each wonton wrapper. Brush edges with a little water; pinch edges together to seal.
3 Shell and devein prawns, leaving tails intact.
4 Bring stock to a boil in large saucepan. Add wontons; cook, uncovered, about 3 minutes or until wontons are just cooked through.
5 Add prawns, remaining sauce, pork and mushrooms; cook, uncovered, until prawns just change in colour. Add buk choy and extra onion; cook, uncovered, until buk choy just wilts.
PER SERVING 9.1g fat; 1155kJ (276 cal)

TIP Uncooked wontons are suitable to freeze for up to three months. You don't have to defrost them; just remove them from the freezer and simmer in stock until cooked through.

beef and vegetable curry

preparation time 10 minutes cooking time 45 minutes serves 4

1 medium brown onion (150g),
chopped finely

⅔ cup (160ml) mild curry paste

1kg beef mince

400g can crushed tomatoes

1 large kumara (500g), coarsely chopped

1 medium eggplant (300g), coarsely chopped

1 cup (250ml) beef stock

1 cup (125g) frozen peas

¼ cup coarsely chopped fresh coriander leaves

1 Combine onion and paste in large microwave-safe dish; cook, covered, on HIGH (100%) 5 minutes, stirring once during cooking.

2 Add beef; cook, covered, on HIGH (100%) 10 minutes, stirring twice during cooking.

3 Add undrained tomatoes, kumara, eggplant and stock; cook, uncovered, on HIGH (100%) 20 minutes, stirring twice during cooking. Add peas; cook, uncovered, on HIGH (100%) 5 minutes. Stir in coriander. Serve with rice, if desired.
PER SERVING *32.4g fat; 2788kJ (667 cal)*

lamb kheema

preparation time 15 minutes cooking time 50 minutes serves 6

2 tablespoons ghee

2 medium brown onions (300g), thinly sliced

2 cloves garlic, crushed

1 tablespoon grated fresh ginger

3 large dried red chillies, crushed

1 tablespoon fennel seeds

2 teaspoons cumin seeds

1 teaspoon ground turmeric

1 teaspoon ground cardamom

3 bay leaves

1kg lamb mince

1 cup (250ml) chicken stock

2 medium tomatoes (380g), chopped

½ cup coarsely chopped fresh mint

1 Heat ghee in large saucepan; cook onion, stirring, until browned. Add garlic, ginger, chillies, seeds, spices and bay leaves to pan; cook, stirring, until fragrant.

2 Add lamb to pan; cook, stirring, until well browned. Add stock, bring to a boil; reduce heat, simmer. Cook, covered, 30 minutes. Cook, uncovered, stirring occasionally, until all liquid has evaporated. Discard bay leaves.

3 Just before serving, add chopped tomatoes and mint to pan; stir until heated through.
PER SERVING *17.6g fat; 1359kJ (325 cal)*

empanadas

preparation time 40 minutes cooking time 45 minutes serves 8

400g can crushed tomatoes

1 tablespoon olive oil

1 medium brown onion (150g), finely chopped

1 clove garlic, crushed

1 teaspoon freshly ground black pepper

½ teaspoon ground cinnamon

½ teaspoon ground cloves

600g beef mince

¼ cup (40g) raisins, chopped coarsely

1 tablespoon cider vinegar

¼ cup (35g) roasted slivered almonds

2 x 800g packages ready-rolled quiche pastry

1 egg, lightly beaten

vegetable oil, for deep-frying

1 Blend or process undrained tomatoes until smooth; reserve.

2 Heat olive oil in large heavy-based saucepan; cook onion, garlic, pepper, cinnamon and cloves, stirring, until onion is soft. Add beef; cook, stirring, until changed in colour. Drain away excess fat from pan. Stir in reserved tomato, raisins and vinegar; simmer, uncovered, about 20 minutes or until filling mixture thickens. Stir in nuts.

3 Cut 9cm rounds from each pastry sheet (you will get 32 rounds). Place a level tablespoon of beef mixture in centre of each round; brush edge with egg. Fold pastry over to enclose filling; press edges together to seal.

4 Heat vegetable oil in large deep frying pan. Deep-fry empanadas until crisp and browned lightly; drain on absorbent paper. Serve immediately with a dollop of sour cream or bottled salsa, if desired.
PER SERVING *26g fat; 1664kJ (398 cal)*

TIP For a lower-fat version, empanadas can be baked, uncovered, in a preheated hot oven about 25 minutes or until browned.

MIDDLE EASTERN TASTES

middle eastern meatballs

preparation time 25 minutes cooking time 20 minutes serves 4

1 tablespoon olive oil

1 large brown onion (200g), finely chopped

2 cloves garlic, crushed

2 teaspoons ground ginger

1 teaspoon ground coriander

2 teaspoons ground cumin

¼ teaspoon ground cinnamon

⅓ cup (50g) dried currants

2 tablespoons finely chopped
fresh coriander

⅓ cup (55g) blanched almonds,
coarsely chopped

1kg beef mince

1 tablespoon sambal oelek

1 cup (70g) stale breadcrumbs

1 egg, lightly beaten

YOGURT SAUCE

1½ cups (375ml) yogurt

2 lebanese cucumbers (260g), seeded,
coarsely chopped

¼ cup finely chopped fresh mint

2 teaspoons lemon juice

1 Combine oil, onion, garlic and ground spices in large microwave-safe dish, cook, uncovered, on HIGH (100%) 5 minutes, stirring once during cooking. Add currants, fresh coriander, nuts, beef, sambal oelek, breadcrumbs and egg; mix well. Shape ¼-cups of mixture into balls.

2 Place meatballs, in single layer, in large oiled shallow microwave-safe dish. Cook, uncovered, in two batches, on HIGH (100%) about 7 minutes or until cooked through. Serve hot or cold meatballs with yogurt sauce.

YOGURT SAUCE Place ingredients in small bowl; mix well.

PER SERVING 35.1g fat; 2934kJ (702 cal)

bucatini with moroccan lamb sauce

preparation time 10 minutes cooking time 20 minutes serves 4

2 teaspoons olive oil

1 small brown onion (80g), finely chopped

2 cloves garlic, crushed

500g lamb mince

1 teaspoon ground cumin

½ teaspoon ground cayenne pepper

½ teaspoon ground cinnamon

2 tablespoons tomato paste

2 x 415g cans crushed tomatoes

1 large zucchini (150g), coarsely chopped

2 tablespoons finely chopped fresh mint leaves

375g bucatini

1 Heat oil in large saucepan; cook onion and garlic, stirring, until onion softens. Add lamb; cook, stirring, until changed in colour. Add spices; cook, stirring, until fragrant.

2 Stir in paste, undrained tomatoes and zucchini; bring to a boil. Reduce heat; simmer, uncovered, about 15 minutes or until sauce thickens slightly. Stir in mint.

3 Meanwhile, cook pasta in large saucepan of boiling water, uncovered, until just tender; drain. Serve pasta topped with sauce.
PER SERVING *11.9g fat; 2357kJ (564 cal)*

kibbeh

preparation time 30 minutes (plus standing time) **cooking time** 20 minutes **makes** 16

1 cup (160g) burghul

600g lamb mince

1 medium brown onion (150g), grated

1 teaspoon ground allspice

1 teaspoon ground oregano

1 tablespoon olive oil

1 tablespoon water

vegetable oil for shallow-frying

FILLING

2 teaspoons olive oil

1 small brown onion (80g), finely chopped

1 tablespoon pine nuts

1 tablespoon slivered almonds

100g lamb mince

½ teaspoon ground allspice

½ teaspoon ground oregano

1 tablespoon finely chopped fresh mint

1 Place burghul in bowl, cover with cold water; stand 15 minutes. Drain burghul, rinse under cold water, drain; squeeze to remove excess moisture.

2 Combine burghul with lamb, onion, allspice, oregano, olive oil and the water in bowl; mix well.

3 Shape ¼-cups of lamb mixture into balls, using damp hands. Hollow out centres of meatballs, using your thumb. Place rounded teaspoons of filling into hollowed centres of meatballs. Shape meatballs into ovals, using damp hands.

4 Heat vegetable oil in large frying pan; shallow-fry kibbeh, in batches, until browned all over and cooked through; drain on absorbent paper.
FILLING Heat oil in medium saucepan, add onion, cook, stirring, until onion is soft. Add nuts; cook, stirring, until lightly browned. Add lamb, allspice and oregano; cook, stirring, until lamb is browned. Stir in mint.
PER KIBBEH *9.1g fat; 648kJ (155 cal)*

lamb kofta

preparation time 20 minutes (plus refrigeration time) cooking time 20 minutes makes 14

750g lamb mince

1 large brown onion (200g), finely chopped

2 cloves garlic, crushed

¼ teaspoon ground cloves

¼ teaspoon ground nutmeg

¼ teaspoon ground hot paprika

½ teaspoon ground cumin

½ teaspoon ground coriander

1 teaspoon finely grated lemon rind

¼ cup (40g) pine nuts, finely chopped

½ cup finely chopped fresh flat-leaf parsley

1 Combine lamb, onion, garlic, spices and rind in bowl; mix well.

2 Add nuts and parsley, mix well; cover, refrigerate 30 minutes.

3 Roll tablespoons of mixture into ovals. Thread ovals onto bamboo skewers, allocating three ovals per skewer.

4 Cook kofta in heated oiled grill pan (or grill or barbecue), in batches, until browned and cooked through.
   PER SKEWER *5.7g fat; 426kJ (102 cal)*

TIP Soak bamboo skewers in water for at least 1 hour to prevent them from burning during cooking.

mexican chilli beef

preparation time 15 minutes cooking time 45 minutes serves 4

1 tablespoon olive oil

1 medium brown onion (150g), coarsely chopped

2 cloves garlic, crushed

1kg beef mince

1 medium jalapeño chilli, finely chopped

400g can crushed tomatoes

1 cup (250ml) beef stock

¾ cup (180ml) tomato paste

425g can Mexican-style baked beans

2 tablespoons coarsely chopped fresh flat-leaf parsley

1 Combine oil, onion and garlic in large microwave-safe dish; cook, uncovered, on HIGH (100%) 4 minutes, stirring once during cooking.

2 Stir in beef; cook, uncovered, on HIGH (100%) 10 minutes, stirring twice. Add chilli, undrained tomatoes, stock and paste. Cook, uncovered, on HIGH (100%) about 25 minutes or until thick, stirring twice.

3 Stir in baked beans; cook, uncovered, on HIGH (100%) 2 minutes. Stir in parsley.
   PER SERVING *22.9g fat; 2312kJ (553 cal)*

lamb pide

preparation time 10 minutes cooking time 20 minutes serves 4

2 small brown onions (160g), finely chopped

2 cloves garlic, crushed

250g lamb mince

1 tablespoon tomato paste

¼ teaspoon hot paprika

1 teaspoon ground cumin

2 small pide

¼ cup (25g) finely grated low-fat
mozzarella cheese

2 tablespoons finely chopped fresh mint

1 Preheat oven to 220°C/200°C fan forced.
2 Cook onion and garlic in lightly oiled medium saucepan, stirring, until onion softens. Add lamb, paste, paprika and cumin; cook, stirring, until lamb is cooked through.
3 Split bread; place bases on oven tray. Spread with lamb mixture; sprinkle with cheese and mint. Replace tops; bake, uncovered, in oven about 10 minutes or until bread is crisp.
   PER SERVING *8.6g fat; 1549kJ (371 cal)*

jacket potatoes

preparation time 15 minutes cooking time 1 hour serves 4

4 large potatoes (1.2kg)

1 tablespoon vegetable oil

500g beef mince

1 medium brown onion (150g),
finely chopped

¼ cup (60ml) tomato paste

½ x 40g packet chicken noodle soup

1½ cups (375ml) water

2 teaspoons Worcestershire sauce

1 medium red capsicum (200g), chopped coarsely

½ medium wombok (750g), finely chopped

2 tablespoons coarsely chopped
fresh flat-leaf parsley

1 Preheat oven to 220°C/200°C fan-forced.
2 Wash and dry potatoes, place on oven tray; bake about 1 hour or until soft.
3 Meanwhile, heat oil in large pan, add beef; cook, stirring, until browned. Add onion; cook, stirring, until onion is soft. Add paste, soup mix, the water, sauce and capsicum; simmer, covered, about 30 minutes or until thickened. Stir in cabbage.
4 Cut a cross in top of each potato; pinch to open slightly. Spoon beef mixture over potatoes; sprinkle with parsley. Serve with leafy green salad, if desired.
   PER SERVING *14g fat; 2149kJ (514 cal)*

ALLSPICE also known as pimento or jamaican pepper; so-named because it tastes like a combination of nutmeg, cumin, clove and cinnamon. Available whole (a dark-brown berry the size of a pea) or ground, and used in both sweet and savoury dishes.

BAY LEAVES aromatic leaves from the bay tree available fresh or dried; used to add a strong, slightly peppery flavour to soups, stocks and casseroles.

BUK CHOY also known as bok choy, pak choi, chinese white cabbage or chinese chard; has a fresh, mild mustard taste. Use both stems and leaves, stir-fried or braised. *Baby buk choy*, also known as pak kat farang or shanghai bok choy, is much smaller and more tender than buk choy. Its mildly acrid, distinctively appealing taste has made it one of the most commonly used Asian greens.

BURGHUL also known as bulghur wheat; hulled steamed wheat kernels that, once dried, are crushed into various size grains. Used in Middle Eastern dishes such as felafel, kibbeh and tabbouleh. Burghul is not the same thing as cracked wheat, the untreated whole wheat berry broken during milling into a cereal product, of varying degrees of coarseness, used in bread making.

CAPSICUM also known as pepper or bell pepper. Native to central and South America; found in red, green, yellow, orange or purplish-black varieties. Membranes and seeds should be discarded before use.

CHEESE
cream commonly known as Philadelphia or Philly; a soft cow-milk cheese. Also available as a spreadable light cream cheese blend.
fontina a smooth, firm Italian cow-milk cheese with a creamy, nutty taste and brown or red rind; ideal for melting or grilling.
parmesan also known as parmigiano, parmesan is a hard, grainy cow-milk cheese which originated in the Parma region of Italy. The curd for this cheese is salted in brine for a month before being aged for up to two years, preferably in humid conditions. Parmesan is grated or flaked and used for pasta, salads and soups; it is also eaten on its own with fruit.

ricotta a soft, sweet, moist, white cow-milk cheese with a low fat content and a slightly grainy texture. The name roughly translates as "cooked again" and refers to ricotta's manufacture from a whey that is itself a by-product of other cheese making.
romano a hard cheese made from sheep's milk, originally produced in Rome, Italy. If you can't find it, use parmesan.

CHILLI FLAKES also sold as crushed chilli. Dehydrated deep-red extremely fine slices and whole seeds; good in cooking or for sprinkling over a dish as one does with salt and pepper.

CHINESE BARBECUED PORK roasted pork fillet with a sweet, sticky coating. Available from Asian food or specialty stores.

CUMIN also known as zeera or comino; cumin is the dried seed of a plant related to the parsley family. Its spicy, almost curry-like flavour is essential to the traditional foods of Mexico, India, North Africa and the Middle East. Available dried as seeds or ground. Black cumin seeds are smaller than standard cumin, and dark brown rather than black; they are mistakenly confused with kalonji.

DASHI the basic fish and seaweed stock that accounts for the distinctive flavour of many Japanese dishes, such as soups and various casserole dishes. Made from dried bonito (a type of tuna) flakes and kombu (kelp); instant dashi (dashi-no-moto) is available in powder, granules and liquid concentrate from Asian food shops.

EGGPLANT also known as aubergine; often thought of as a vegetable but is actually a fruit and belongs to the same family as the tomato, chilli and potato. Ranging in size from tiny to very large and in colour from pale green to deep purple. Can be purchased char-grilled, packed in oil, in jars.
finger also known as baby or japanese eggplant; very small and slender so can be used without disgorging.

GALANGAL also known as ka or lengkaus if fresh, and laos if dried and powdered; a root similar to ginger in its use. Having a hot, sour ginger-citrusy flavour; used in fish curries and soups.

GARAM MASALA literally meaning blended spices in its northern Indian place of origin; based on varying proportions of cardamom, cinnamon, cloves, coriander, fennel and cumin, roasted and ground together. Black pepper and chilli can be added for a hotter version.

GHEE clarified butter (the milk solids are removed); this fat has a high smoking point so can be heated to a high temperature without burning. Used as a cooking medium in most Indian recipes.

GOW GEE PASTRY made of flour, egg and water; found in the refrigerated or freezer section of Asian food shops and many supermarkets. These come in different thicknesses and shapes. Thin wrappers work best in soups, while the thicker ones are best for frying; and the choice of round or square, small or large is dependent on the recipe.

KAFFIR LIME LEAVES also known as bai magrood; look like two glossy dark green leaves joined end to end, forming a rounded hourglass shape. Used fresh or dried in many South-East Asian dishes, they are used like bay leaves or curry leaves, especially in Thai cooking. Sold fresh, dried or frozen, the dried leaves are less potent, so double the number if using them as a substitute for fresh; a strip of fresh lime peel may be substituted for each kaffir lime leaf.

KECAP MANIS a dark, thick sweet soy sauce used in most South-East Asian cuisines. Depending on the manufacturer, the sauces' sweetness is derived from the addition of either molasses or palm sugar when brewed. Use as a condiment, dipping sauce, ingredient or marinade.

KUMARA the Polynesian name of an orange-fleshed sweet potato often confused with yam.

LEBANESE CUCUMBER short, slender and thin-skinned. Probably the most popular variety because of its tender, edible skin, tiny, yielding seeds and sweet, fresh and flavoursome taste.

LAMINGTON PAN 20cm x 30cm slab cake pan, 3cm deep.

GLOSSARY

LETTUCE

butter small, round, loosely formed heads with a sweet flavour; soft, buttery-textured leaves range from pale green on the outer leaves to pale yellow-green inner leaves.

oak leaf also known as feuille de chene; curly-leafed but not as frizzy as the coral lettuce. Has crunchy stems and tender leaves. Found in both red and green varieties.

MUSHROOMS

button small, cultivated white mushrooms with a mild flavour. When a recipe in this book calls for an unspecified type of mushroom, use button.

shiitake fresh, are also known as chinese black, forest or golden oak mushrooms. Although cultivated, they have the earthiness and taste of wild mushrooms. Large and meaty, they can be used as a substitute for meat in some Asian vegetarian dishes.

MIRIN a Japanese champagne-coloured cooking wine, made of glutinous rice and alcohol. It is used expressly for cooking and should not be confused with sake.

MUSTARD SEEDS

black also known as brown mustard seeds; more pungent than the white variety; used frequently in curries.

yellow also known as white mustard seeds; used ground for mustard powder and in most prepared mustards.

ONIONS

green also known as scallion or, incorrectly, shallot; an immature onion picked before the bulb has formed, having a long, bright-green edible stalk.

red also known as spanish, red spanish or bermuda onion; a sweet-flavoured, large, purple-red onion.

PALM SUGAR also known as nam tan pip, jaggery, jawa or gula melaka; made from the sap of the sugar palm tree. Light brown to black in colour and usually sold in rock-hard cakes; substitute with brown sugar if unavailable.

PAPRIKA ground dried sweet red capsicum (bell pepper); there are many grades and types available, including sweet, hot, mild and smoked.

POLENTA also known as cornmeal; a flour-like cereal made of dried corn (maize); also the name of the dish made from it.

PRAWNS also known as shrimp. Varieties include, school, king, royal red, sydney harbour, tiger. Can be bought uncooked (green) or cooked, with or without shells.

PROSCIUTTO a kind of unsmoked Italian ham; salted, air-cured and aged, it is usually eaten uncooked. There are many styles of prosciutto, one of the best being Parma ham, from Italy's Emilia Romagna region.

RICE VERMICELLI also known as sen mee, mei fun or bee hoon. Used throughout Asia in spring rolls and cold salads; similar to bean threads, only longer and made with rice flour instead of mung bean starch. Before using, soak the dried noodles in hot water until softened, boil them briefly then rinse with hot water. Vermicelli can also be deep-fried until crunchy and then used in a Chinese chicken salad, or as a garnish or bed for sauces.

ROCKET also known as arugula, rugula and rucola; peppery green leaf eaten raw in salads or used in cooking. *Baby rocket leaves* are smaller and less peppery.

SAKE Japan's favourite wine, made from fermented rice, is used for marinating, cooking and as part of dipping sauces. If sake is unavailable, dry sherry, vermouth or brandy can be substituted. If drinking sake, stand it first in a container in hot water for 20 minutes to warm it through.

SAMBAL OELEK (also ulek or olek), Indonesian in origin, this is a salty paste made from ground chillies and vinegar.

SHALLOTS

purple also known as Asian shallots; related to the onion but resembling garlic (they grow in bulbs of multiple cloves). Thin-layered and intensely flavoured, they are used in cooking throughout South-East Asia.

fried served as a condiment on Asian tables to be sprinkled over just-cooked food. Found in cellophane bags or jars at all Asian food shops; once opened, they will keep for months if stored tightly sealed. Make your own by frying thinly sliced peeled shallots or baby onions until golden brown and crisp.

SILKEN TOFU not a type of tofu but reference to the manufacturing process of straining soybean liquid through silk; this denotes best quality.

SILVER BEET also known as swiss chard and, incorrectly, spinach, has fleshy stalks and large leaves.

SNOW PEAS also called "mange tout"; a variety of garden pea, eaten pod and all (though you may need to trim the ends). Used in stir-fries or eaten raw in salads. Snow pea sprouts are available from supermarkets or greengrocers and are usually eaten raw in salads or sandwiches.

SOBA thin, pale-brown noodle originally from Japan; made from buckwheat and varying proportions of wheat flour. Available dried and fresh, and in flavoured varieties (for instance, green tea), eaten in soups, stir-fries and, chilled, on their own.

TURKISH BREAD also known as pide. Sold in long (about 45cm) flat loaves as well as individual rounds; made from wheat flour and sprinkled with black onion seeds (kalonji).

TURMERIC also known as kamin; is a rhizome related to galangal and ginger. Must be grated or pounded to release its somewhat acrid aroma and pungent flavour. Known for the golden colour it imparts, fresh turmeric can be substituted with the more common dried powder.

VIETNAMESE MINT not a mint at all, but a pungent and peppery narrow-leafed member of the buckwheat family. Not confined to Vietnam, it is also known as Cambodian mint, pak pai (Thailand), laksa leaf (Indonesia), daun kesom (Singapore) and rau ram in Vietnam. It is a common ingredient in Thai foods, particularly soups, salads and stir-fries.

WITLOF also known as belgian endive; related to and confused with chicory. A versatile vegetable, it tastes as good cooked as it does eaten raw. Grown in darkness like white asparagus to prevent it becoming green; it looks somewhat like a tightly furled, cream to very light-green cigar. The leaves can be removed and used to hold a canapé filling; the whole vegetable can be opened up, stuffed then baked or casseroled; and the leaves can be tossed in a salad with other vegetables.

WOMBOK also known as chinese cabbage, peking or napa cabbage; elongated in shape with pale green, crinkly leaves, this is the most common cabbage in South-East Asia, forming the basis of the pickled Korean condiment, kim chi. Can be shredded or chopped and eaten raw or braised, steamed or stir-fried.

ZUCCHINI also known as courgette; a small, pale- or dark-green, yellow or white vegetable belonging to the squash family. Harvested when young, its edible flowers can be stuffed with a mild cheese or other similarly delicate ingredients then deep-fried or oven-baked to make a delicious appetiser. Good cored and stuffed with various meat or rice fillings; in Italian vegetable dishes and pasta sauces; and as one of the vegetables that make ratatouille.

MEASURES

One Australian metric measuring cup holds approximately 250ml; one Australian metric tablespoon holds 20ml; one Australian metric teaspoon holds 5ml.

The difference between one country's measuring cups and another's is within a two- or three-teaspoon variance, and will not affect your cooking results. North America, New Zealand and the United Kingdom use a 15ml tablespoon.

All cup and spoon measurements are level. The most accurate way of measuring dry ingredients is to weigh them. When measuring liquids, use a clear glass or plastic jug with the metric markings.

We use large eggs with an average weight of 60g.

DRY MEASURES

METRIC	IMPERIAL
15g	½oz
30g	1oz
60g	2oz
90g	3oz
125g	4oz (¼lb)
155g	5oz
185g	6oz
220g	7oz
250g	8oz (½lb)
280g	9oz
315g	10oz
345g	11oz
375g	12oz (¾lb)
410g	13oz
440g	14oz
470g	15oz
500g	16oz (1lb)
750g	24oz (1½lb)
1kg	32oz (2lb)

LIQUID MEASURES

METRIC	IMPERIAL
30ml	1 fluid oz
60ml	2 fluid oz
100ml	3 fluid oz
125ml	4 fluid oz
150ml	5 fluid oz (¼ pint/1 gill)
190ml	6 fluid oz
250ml	8 fluid oz
300ml	10 fluid oz (½ pint)
500ml	16 fluid oz
600ml	20 fluid oz (1 pint)
1000ml (1 litre)	1¾ pints

LENGTH MEASURES

METRIC	IMPERIAL
3mm	⅛in
6mm	¼in
1cm	½in
2cm	¾in
2.5cm	1in
5cm	2in
6cm	2½in
8cm	3in
10cm	4in
13cm	5in
15cm	6in
18cm	7in
20cm	8in
23cm	9in
25cm	10in
28cm	11in
30cm	12in (1ft)

OVEN TEMPERATURES

These oven temperatures are only a guide for conventional ovens. For fan-forced ovens, check the manufacturer's manual.

	°C (CELSIUS)	°F (FAHRENHEIT)	GAS MARK
Very slow	120	250	½
Slow	150	275-300	1-2
Moderately slow	160	325	3
Moderate	180	350-375	4-5
Moderately hot	200	400	6
Hot	220	425-450	7-8
Very hot	240	475	9

CONVERSION CHART

A

avocado cream 19

B

bacon and beef loaf with
   plum sauce 29
bean and beef stew with
   polenta wedges 55
beef and bacon loaf with
   plum sauce 29
beef and bean stew with
   polenta wedges 55
beef and pine nut pastries,
   minted 34
beef and silver beet burgers 7
beef and vegetable curry 100
beef burgers, gourmet 4
beef kofta 76
beef, mexican chilli 110
beef pizza, spicy 48
beef, tomato and pea pies 22
bolognese jaffles 51
bolognese, rigatoni 56
bolognese, spaghetti 39
bubble and squeak pie 25
bucatini with moroccan
   lamb sauce 106
burgers, beef and silver beet 7
burgers, cajun chicken 19
burgers, chicken and ham 15
burgers, chicken, with
   avocado cream 19
burgers, country-style 20
burgers, fish 15
burgers, lamb, with tomato salsa 16
burgers, mexican 7
burgers, pork chutney 11
burgers with mustard
   mayonnaise 8

C

cajun chicken burgers 19
cannelloni, chicken and
   prosciutto 36
caramelised onion,
   meatloaf with 33

casserole, mince and macaroni 51
cheese and spinach meatloaves,
   individual 25
cheese sauce 47
chicken and ham burgers 15
chicken and prosciutto
   cannelloni 36
chicken and spinach lasagne 43
chicken burgers with
   avocado cream 19
chicken burgers, cajun 19
chicken, pork and rice noodle
   stir-fry 87
chicken salad in witlof, spicy 88
chicken, spicy thai-style 95
chicken stir-fry noodles 64
chilli con carne pie 26
chilli, mint and beef filling 30
chilli mushroom sauce,
   meatballs with 63
chilli tomato sauce 12
chutney burgers, pork 11
coconut milk, spicy, meatballs in 83
combination wonton soup 99
country-style burgers 20
cracked wheat and minced
   beef lasagne 43
cream, avocado 19
crispy fried noodles with
   pork and prawn 71
curry, beef and vegetable 100
curry, kofta 72
curry, nepalese pork mince 67
curry, red, fish ball and green
   peppercorn 91

D

dipping sauce 15
dumplings, pan-fried 96

E

empanadas 102

F

fettuccine with meatballs in
   rosemary paprika sauce 52

filling, chilli, mint and beef 30
filling (kibbeh) 109
filling, kumara and coriander 30
fish ball and green peppercorn
   red curry 91
fish burgers 15
fried soba 84
frypan pizza 60

G

gourmet beef burgers 4
gravy, tomato 29
green peppercorn red curry,
   fish ball and 91
gyoza with soy vinegar sauce 75

H

ham and chicken burgers 15
herbs, fresh, savoury mince with 60
homemade sausage rolls 33

I

individual cheese and
   spinach meatloaves 25

J

jacket potatoes 113
jaffles, bolognese 51

K

kashmiri lamb kofta 92
kibbeh 109
kofta, beef 76
kofta curry 72
kofta, kashmiri lamb 92
kofta, lamb 110
kofta, lamb, with chilli and
   yogurt sauces 12
kumara and coriander filling 30

L

lamb and burghul sausages 11
lamb burgers with tomato salsa 16

ARE YOU MISSING SOME OF THE WORLD'S FAVOURITE COOKBOOKS?

The Australian Women's Weekly Cookbooks are available from bookshops, cookshops, supermarkets and other stores all over the world. You can also buy direct from the publisher, using the order form below.

ACP Magazines Ltd Privacy Notice
This book may contain offers, competitions or surveys that require you to provide information about yourself if you choose to enter or take part in any such Reader Offer. If you provide information about yourself to ACP Magazines Ltd, the company will use this information to provide you with the products or services you have requested, and may supply your information to contractors that help ACP to do this. ACP will also use your information to inform you of other ACP publications, products, services and events. ACP will also give your information to organisations that are providing special prizes or offers, and that are clearly associated with the Reader Offer. Unless you tell us not to, we may give your information to other organisations that use it to inform you about other products, services and events or who may give it to other organisations that may use it for this purpose. If you would like to gain access to the information ACP holds about you, please contact ACP's Privacy Officer at ACP Magazines Ltd, 54-58 Park Street, Sydney, NSW 2000, Australia.

☐ **Privacy Notice** Please do not provide information about me to any organisation not associated with this offer.

To order: Mail or fax – photocopy or complete the order form above, and send your credit card details or cheque payable to: Australian Consolidated Press (UK), ACP Books, 10 Scirocco Close, Moulton Park Office Village, Northampton NN3 6AP
phone (+44) (0)1604 642200
fax (+44) (0)1604 642300
email books@acpuk.com
or order online at www.acpuk.com
Non-UK residents: We accept the credit cards listed on the coupon, or cheques, drafts or International Money Orders payable in sterling and drawn on a UK bank. Credit card charges are at the exchange rate current at the time of payment.
Postage and packing UK: Add £1.00 per order plus £1.75 per book.
Postage and packing overseas: Add £2.00 per order plus £3.50 per book. All pricing current at time of going to press and subject to change/availability.
Offer ends 31.12.2008

TITLE	RRP	QTY	TITLE	RRP	QTY
100 Fast Fillets	£6.99		Indian Cooking Class	£6.99	
After Work Fast	£6.99		Japanese Cooking Class	£6.99	
Beginners Cooking Class	£6.99		Just For One	£6.99	
Beginners Thai	£6.99		Just For Two	£6.99	
Best Food Desserts	£6.99		Kids' Birthday Cakes	£6.99	
Best Food Fast	£6.99		Kids Cooking	£6.99	
Breads & Muffins	£6.99		Kids' Cooking Step-by-Step	£6.99	
Cafe Classics	£6.99		Low-carb, Low-fat	£6.99	
Cakes Bakes & Desserts	£6.99		Low-fat Feasts	£6.99	
Cakes Biscuits & Slices	£6.99		Low-fat Food for Life	£6.99	
Cakes Cooking Class	£6.99		Low-fat Meals in Minutes	£6.99	
Caribbean Cooking	£6.99		Main Course Salads	£6.99	
Casseroles	£6.99		Mexican	£6.99	
Casseroles & Slow-Cooked Classics	£6.99		Middle Eastern Cooking Class	£6.99	
Cheap Eats	£6.99		Mince in Minutes	£6.99	
Cheesecakes. baked and chilled	£6.99		Moroccan & the Foods of North Africa	£6.99	
Chicken	£6.99		Muffins, Scones & Breads	£6.99	
Chicken Meals in Minutes	£6.99		New Casseroles	£6.99	
Chinese & the foods of Thailand, Vietnam, Malaysia & Japan	£6.99		New Curries	£6.99	
			New Finger Food	£6.99	
Chinese Cooking Class	£6.99		New French Food	£6.99	
Christmas Cooking	£6.99		New Salads	£6.99	
Chocolate	£6.99		Party Food and Drink	£6.99	
Chocs & Treats	£6.99		Pasta Meals in Minutes	£6.99	
Cocktails	£6.99		Potatoes	£6.99	
Cookies & Biscuits	£6.99		Rice & Risotto	£6.99	
Cupcakes & Fairycakes	£6.99		Salads: Simple, Fast & Fresh	£6.99	
Detox	£6.99		Sauces Salsas & Dressings	£6.99	
Dinner Lamb	£6.99		Sensational Stir-Fries	£6.99	
Dinner Seafood	£6.99		Simple Healthy Meals	£6.99	
Easy Curry	£6.99		Soup	£6.99	
Easy Midweek Meals	£6.99		Stir-fry	£6.99	
Easy Spanish-Style	£6.99		Superfoods for Exam Success	£6.99	
Essential Soup	£6.99		Sweet Old-Fashioned Favourites	£6.99	
Food for Fit and Healthy Kids	£6.99		Tapas Mezze Antipasto & other bites	£6.99	
Foods of the Mediterranean	£6.99		Thai Cooking Class	£6.99	
Foods That Fight Back	£6.99		Traditional Italian	£6.99	
Fresh Food Fast	£6.99		Vegetarian Meals in Minutes	£6.99	
Fresh Food for Babies & Toddlers	£6.99		Vegie Food	£6.99	
Good Food for Babies & Toddlers	£6.99		Wicked Sweet Indulgences	£6.99	
Greek Cooking Class	£6.99		Wok, Meals in Minutes	£6.99	
Grills	£6.99				
Healthy Heart Cookbook	£6.99		TOTAL COST:	£	

Mr/Mrs/Ms _____

Address _____

_____ Postcode _____

Day time phone _____ email* (optional) _____

I enclose my cheque/money order for £ _____

or please charge £ _____

to my: ☐ Access   ☐ Mastercard   ☐ Visa   ☐ Diners Club

Card number ⌷⌷⌷⌷ ⌷⌷⌷⌷ ⌷⌷⌷⌷ ⌷⌷⌷⌷

Expiry date _____ 3 digit security code *(found on reverse of card)* _____

Cardholder's name_____ Signature _____

* By including your email address, you consent to receipt of any email regarding this magazine, and other emails which inform you of ACP's other publications, products, services and events, and to promote third party goods and services you may be interested in.

You'll find these books and more available on sale at bookshops, cookshops, selected supermarkets or direct from the publisher (see order form page 119).

TEST KITCHEN

Food director Pamela Clark

Test Kitchen manager Kellie-Marie Thomas

Nutritional information Belinda Farlow

ACP BOOKS

Editorial director Susan Tomnay

Creative director Hieu Chi Nguyen

Designer Caryl Wiggins

Director of sales Brian Cearnes

Marketing manager Bridget Cody

Business analyst Ashley Davies

Chief executive officer Ian Law

Group publisher Pat Ingram

General manager Christine Whiston

Editorial director (WW) Deborah Thomas

RIGHTS ENQUIRIES

Laura Bamford, Director ACP Books

lbamford@acpuk.com

Produced by ACP Books, Sydney.

Printed by Dai Nippon, c/o Samhwa Printing Co., Ltd, 237-10 Kuro-Dong, Kuro-Ku, Seoul, Korea.

Published by ACP Books, a division of ACP Magazines Ltd, 54 Park St, Sydney; GPO Box 4088, Sydney, NSW 2001. Ph: (02) 9282 8618 Fax: (02) 9267 9438. acpbooks@acpmagazines.com.au www.acpbooks.com.au

To order books, phone 136 116 (within Australia). Send recipe enquiries to: recipeenquiries@acpmagazines.com.au

Australia Distributed by Network Services, phone +61 2 9282 8777 fax +61 2 9264 3278 networkweb@networkservicescompany.com.au

United Kingdom Distributed by Australian Consolidated Press (UK), phone (01604) 642 200 fax (01604) 642 300 books@acpuk.com

New Zealand Distributed by Netlink Distribution Company, phone (9) 366 9966 ask@ndc.co.nz

South Africa Distributed by PSD Promotions, phone (27 11) 392 6065/7 fax (27 11) 392 6079/80 orders@psdprom.co.za

Mince in minutes: the Australian womens weekly Includes index.

ISBN 978 1 86396 718 1 (pbk)

1. Cookery (Meat). 2. Mincemeat.

3. Quick and easy cookery.

I. Clark, Pamela.

II. Title: Australian women's weekly.

641.66

© ACP Magazines Ltd 2007

ABN 18 053 273 546